# THiS BOOK BELONGS TO:

_____

_____

_____

# COLOR TEST PAGE

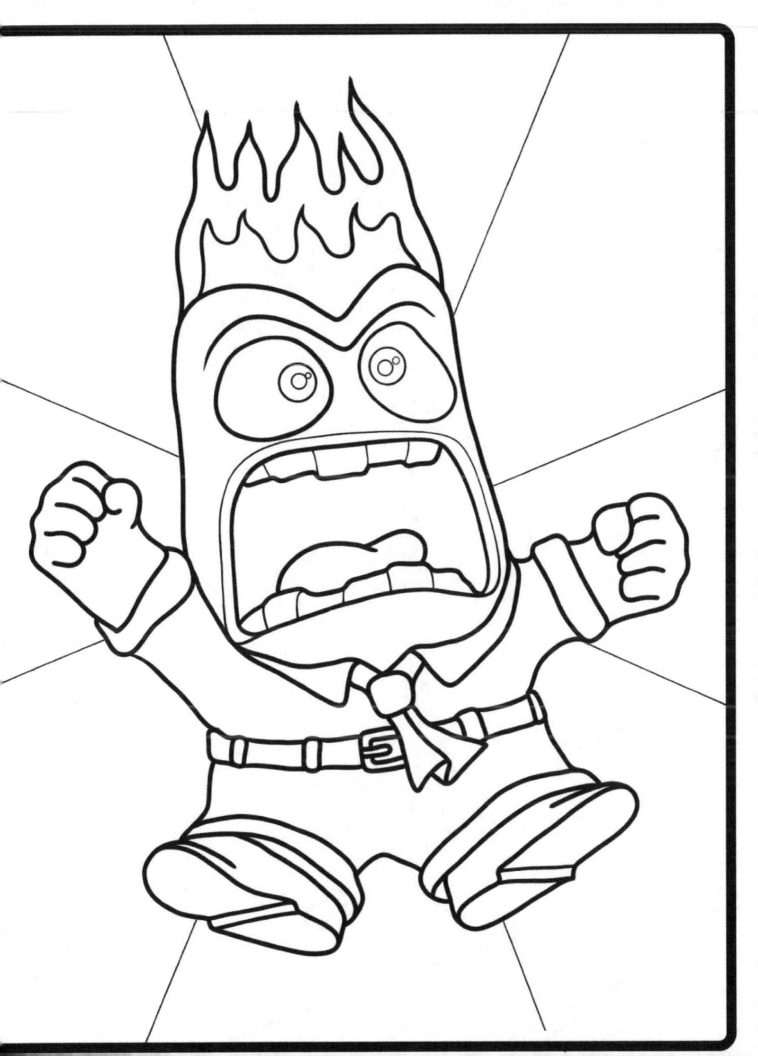

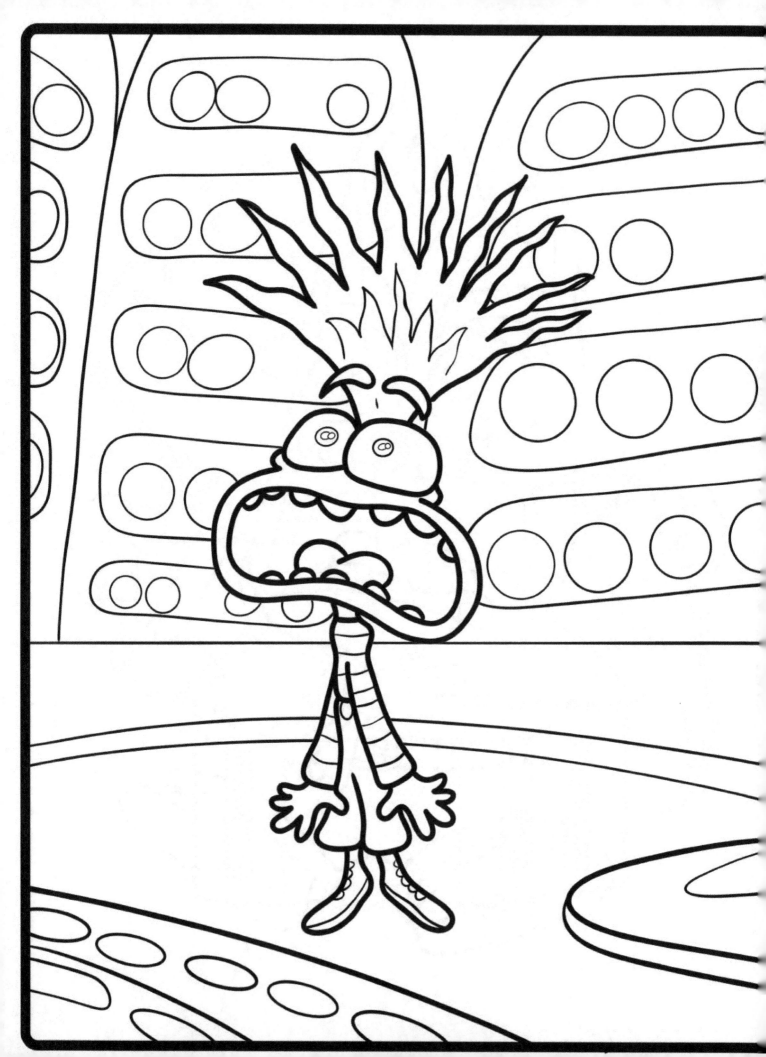

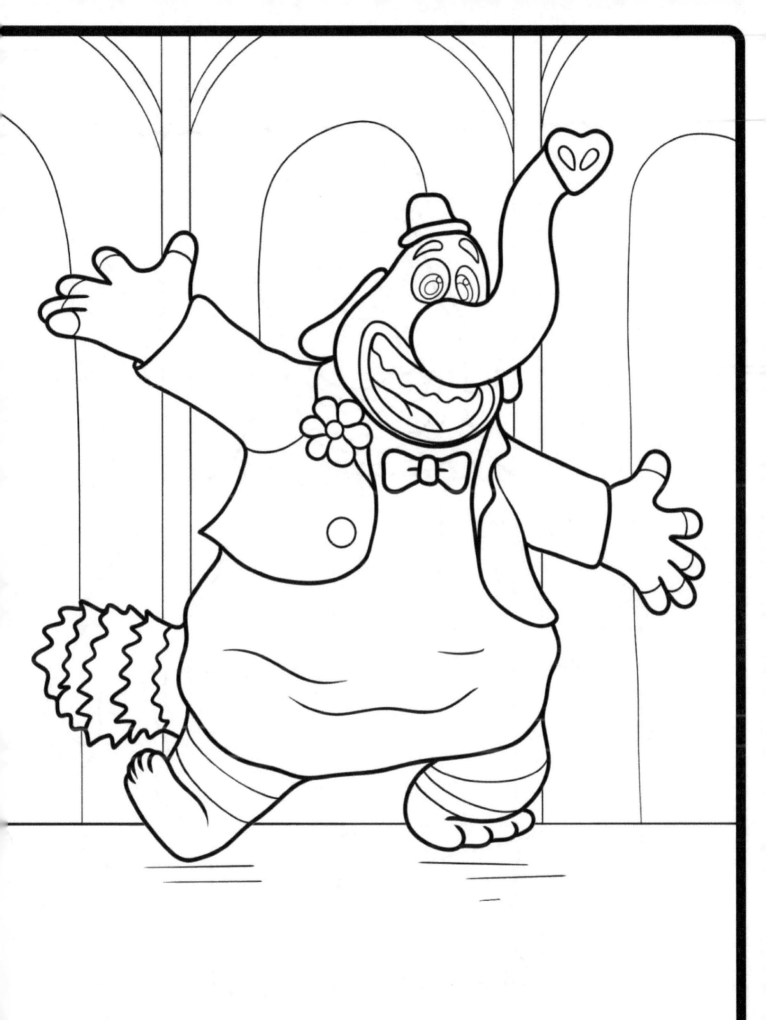

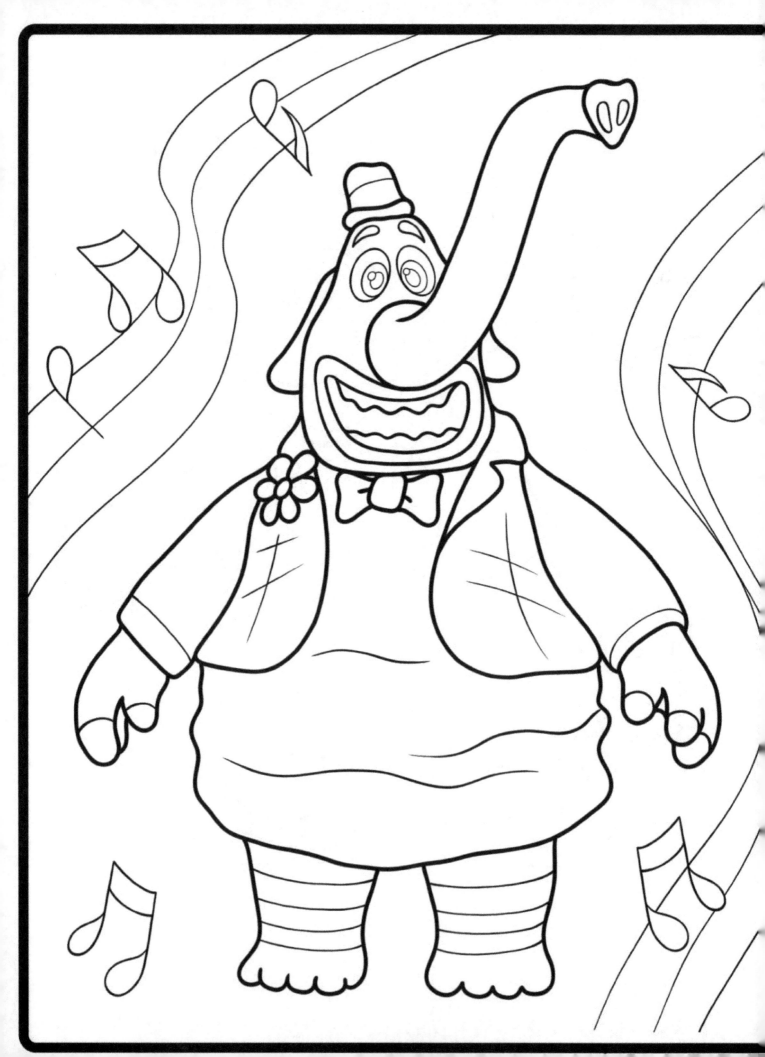

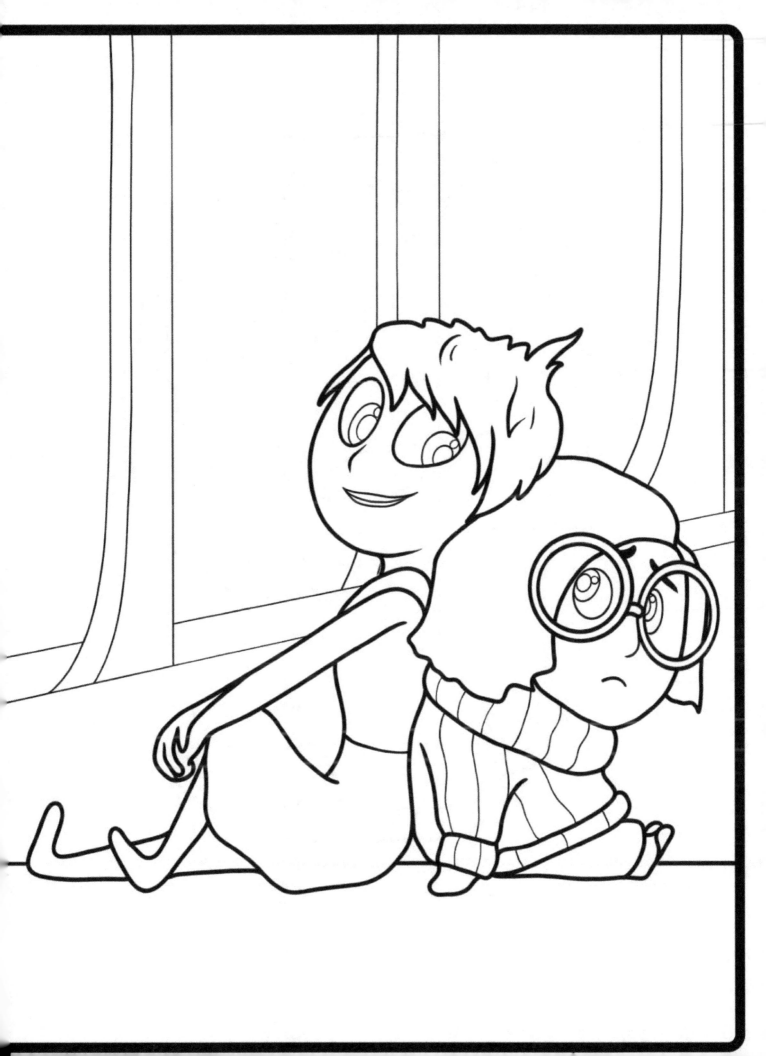

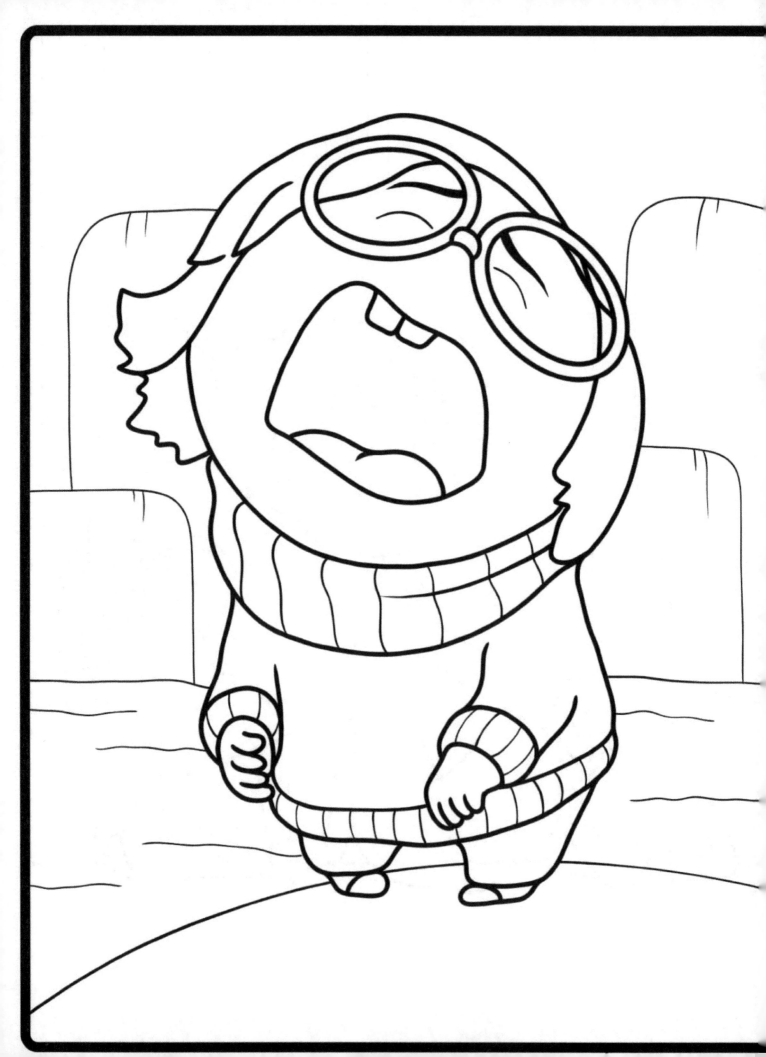

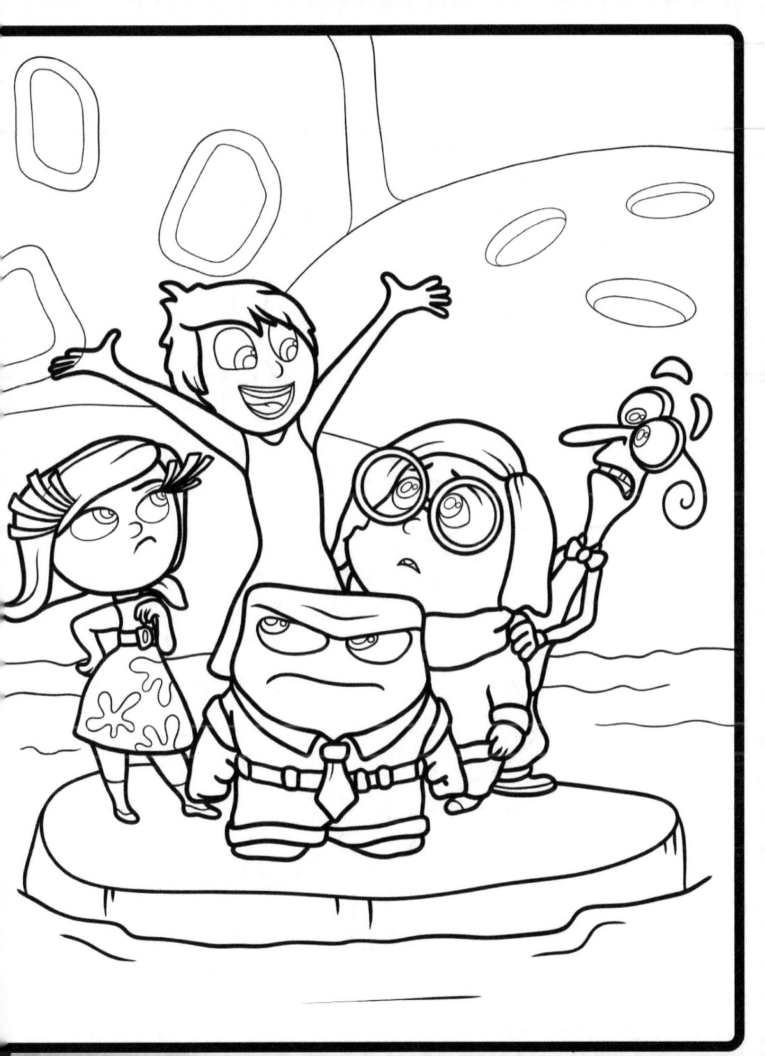

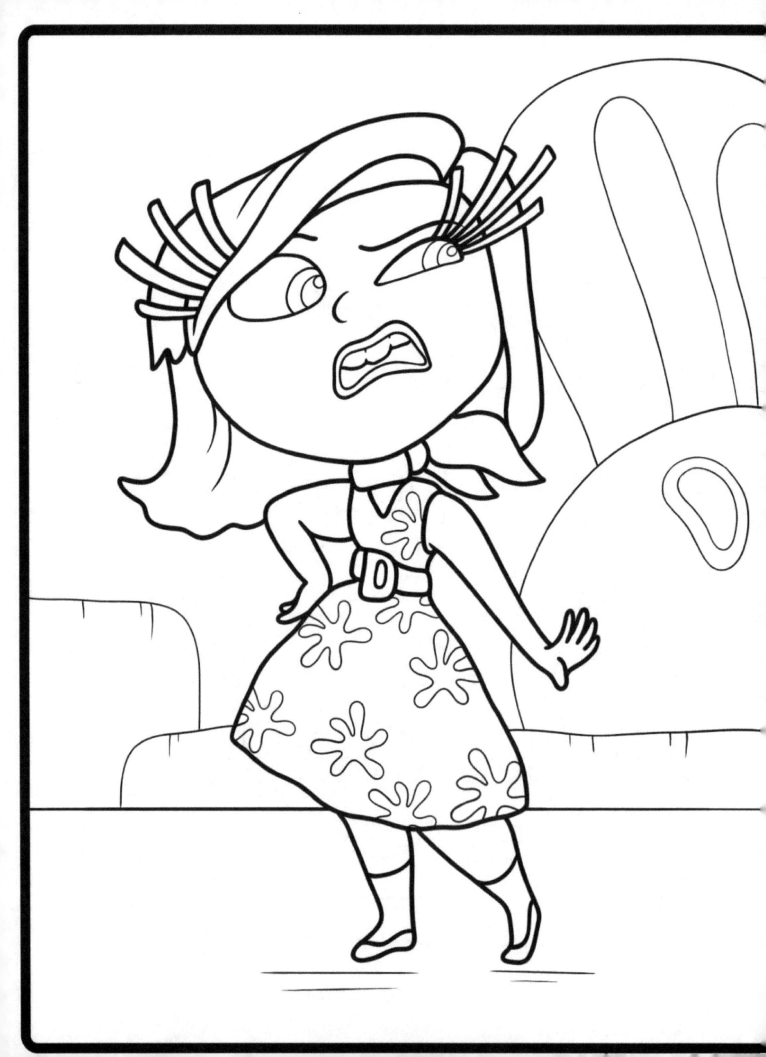

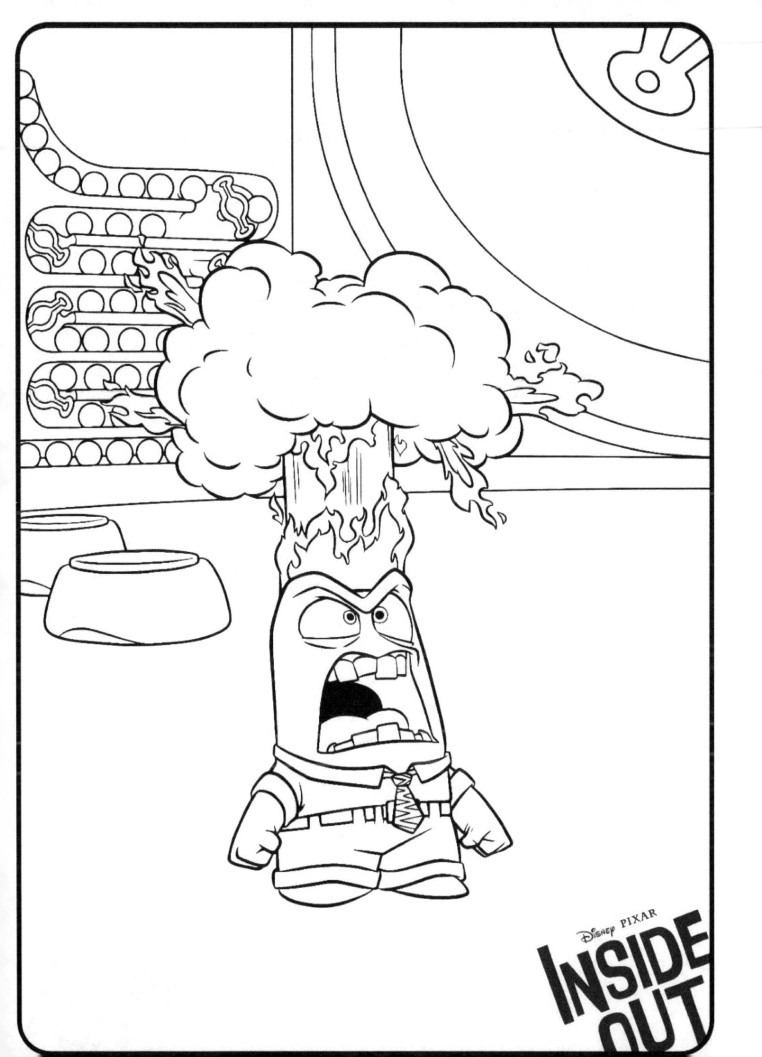

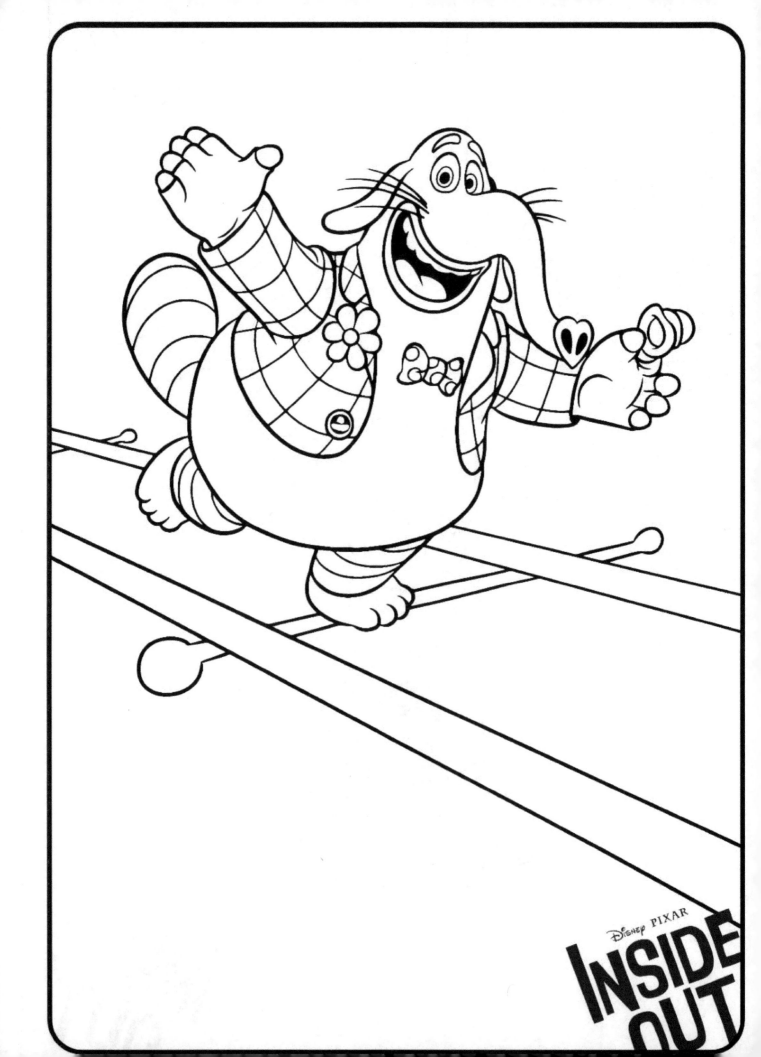

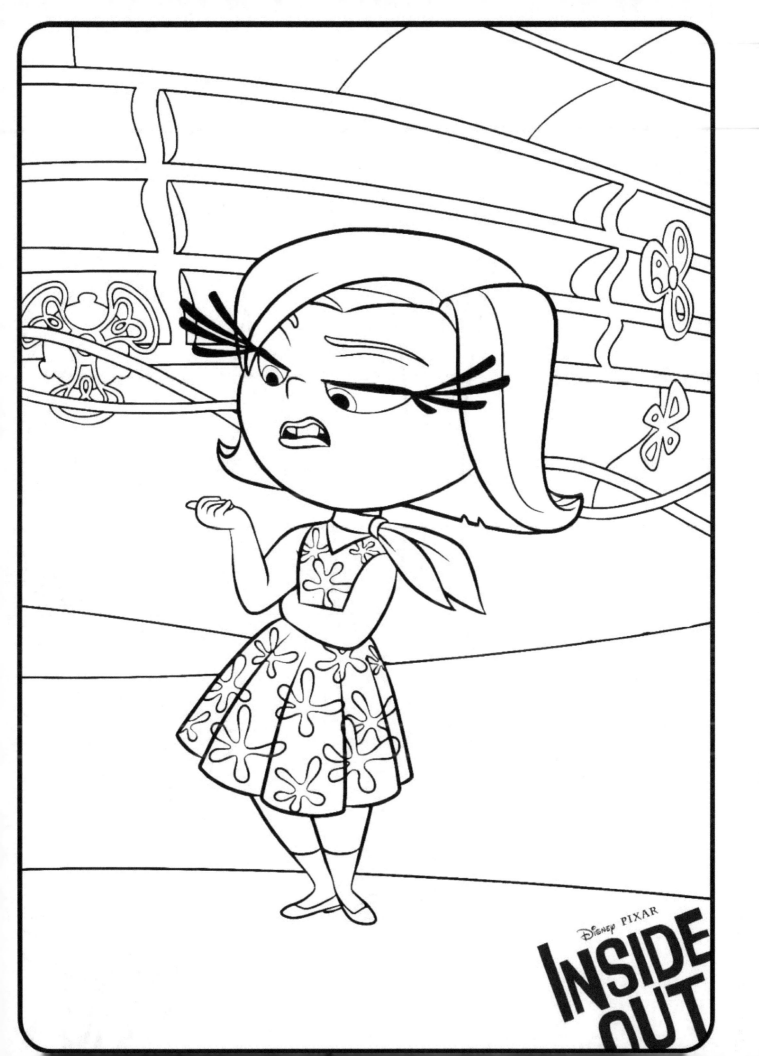

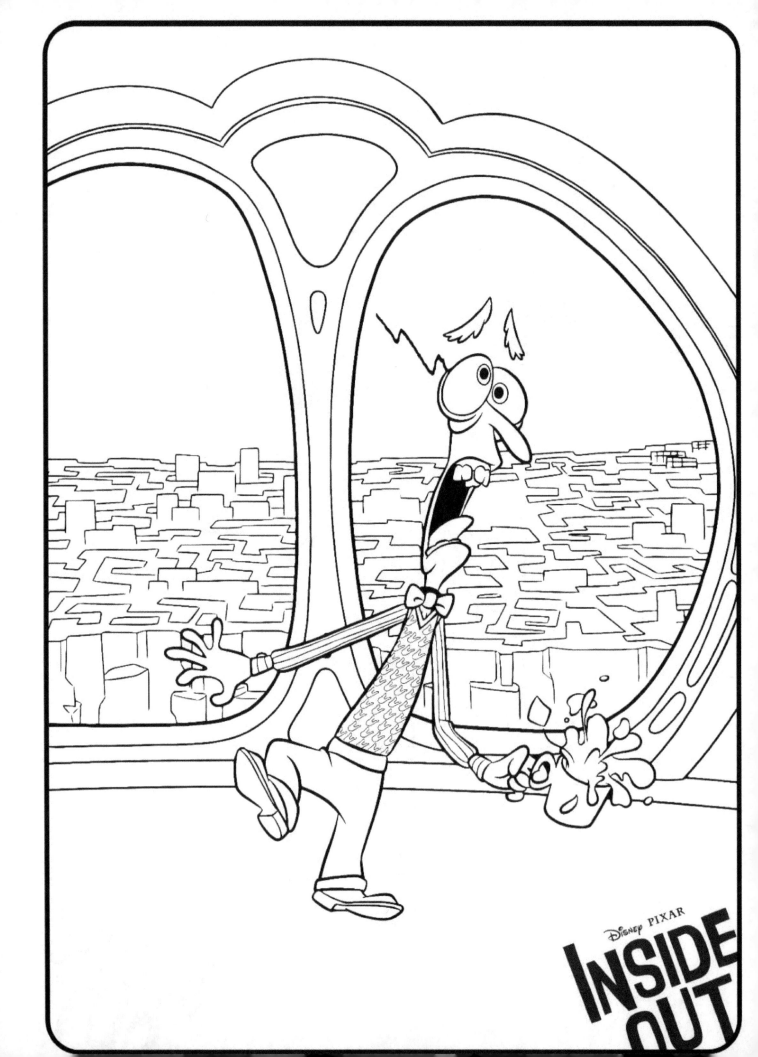

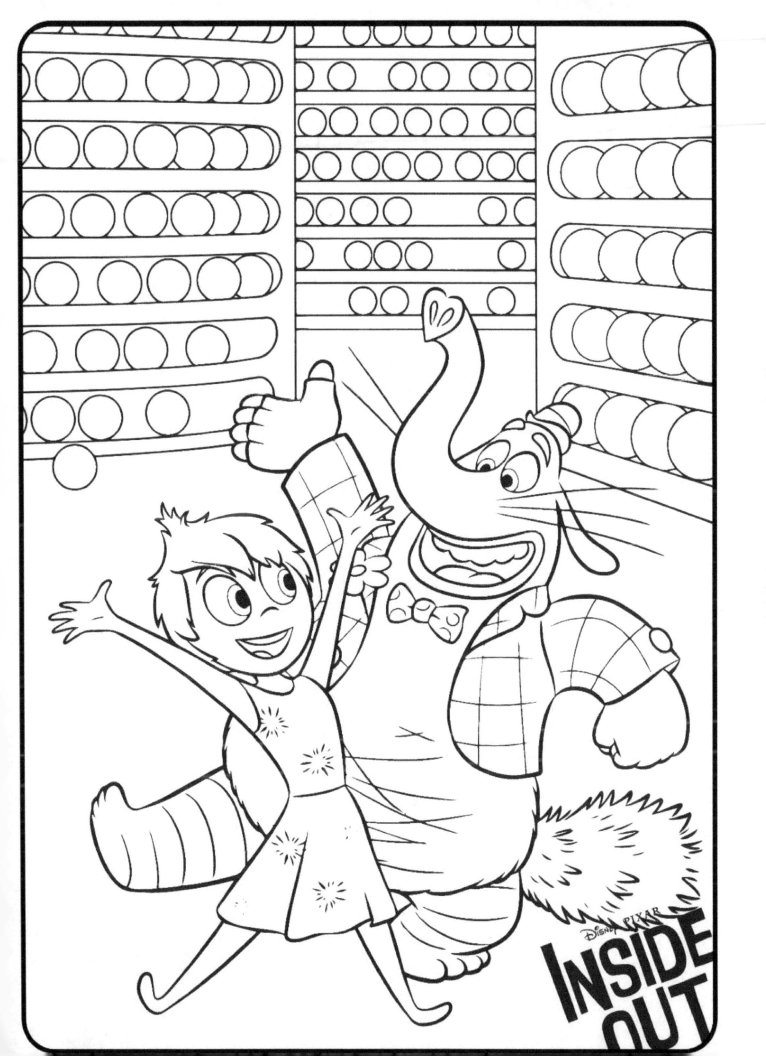

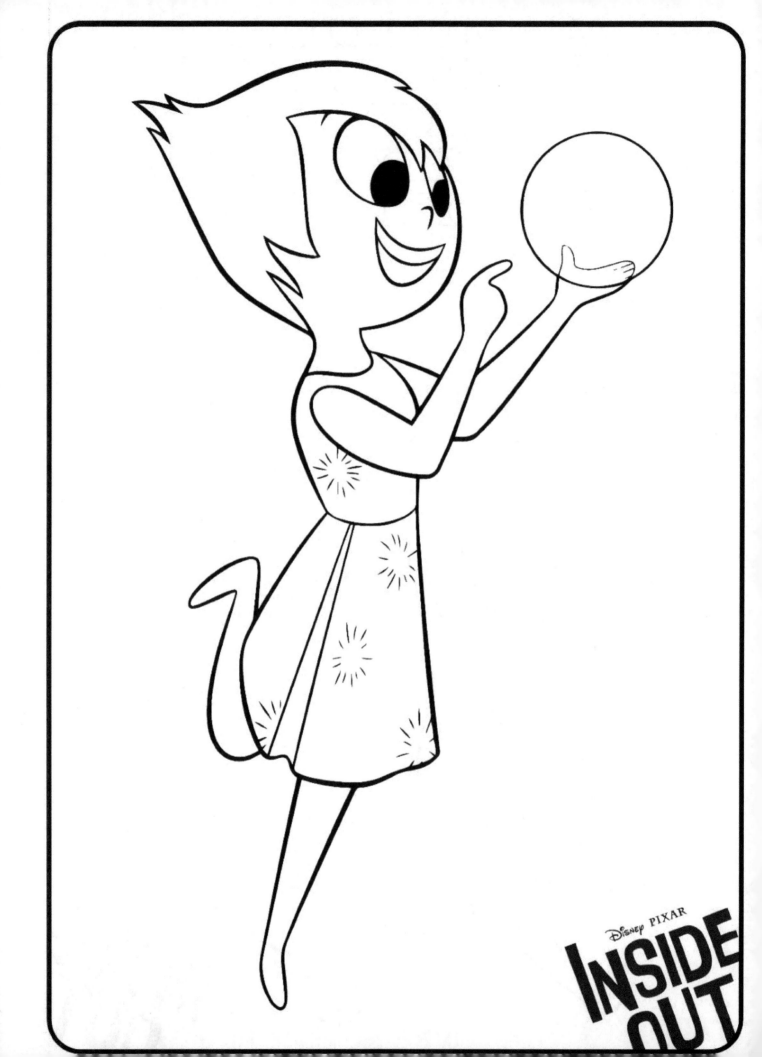

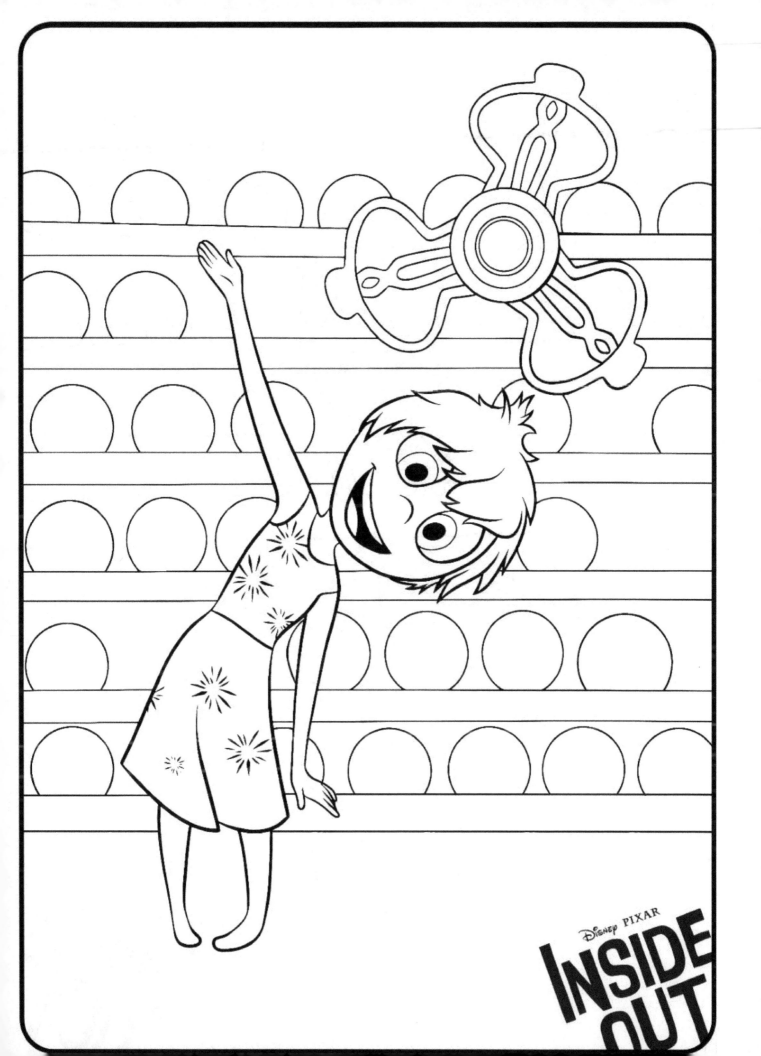

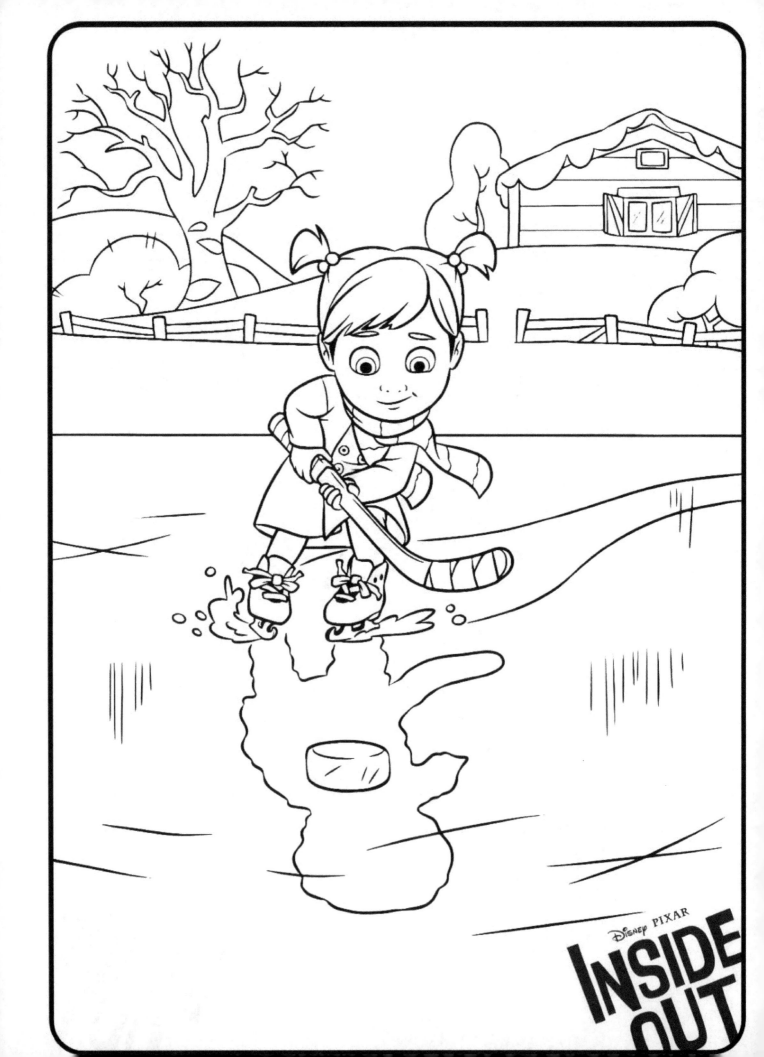

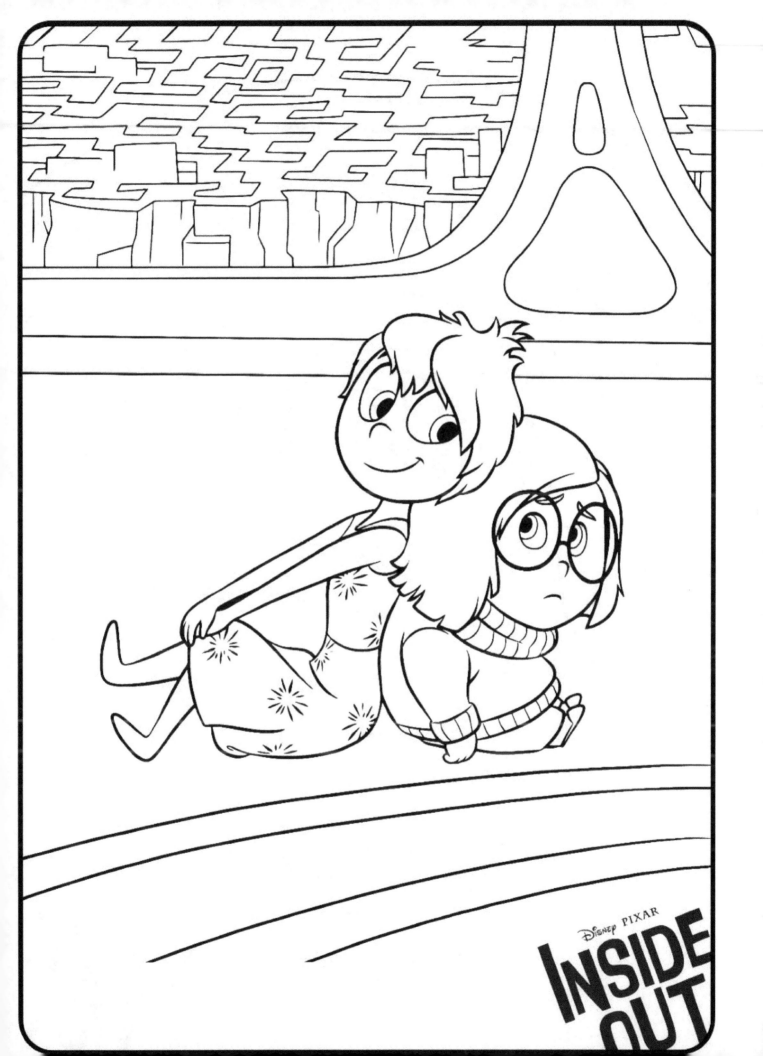

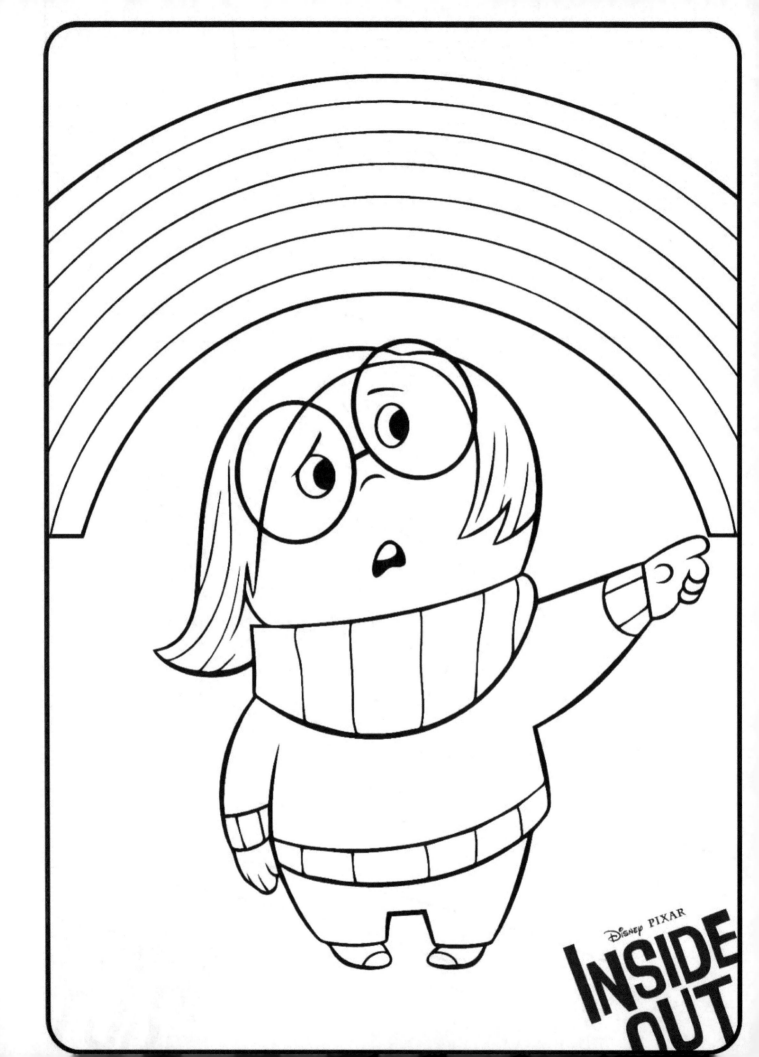

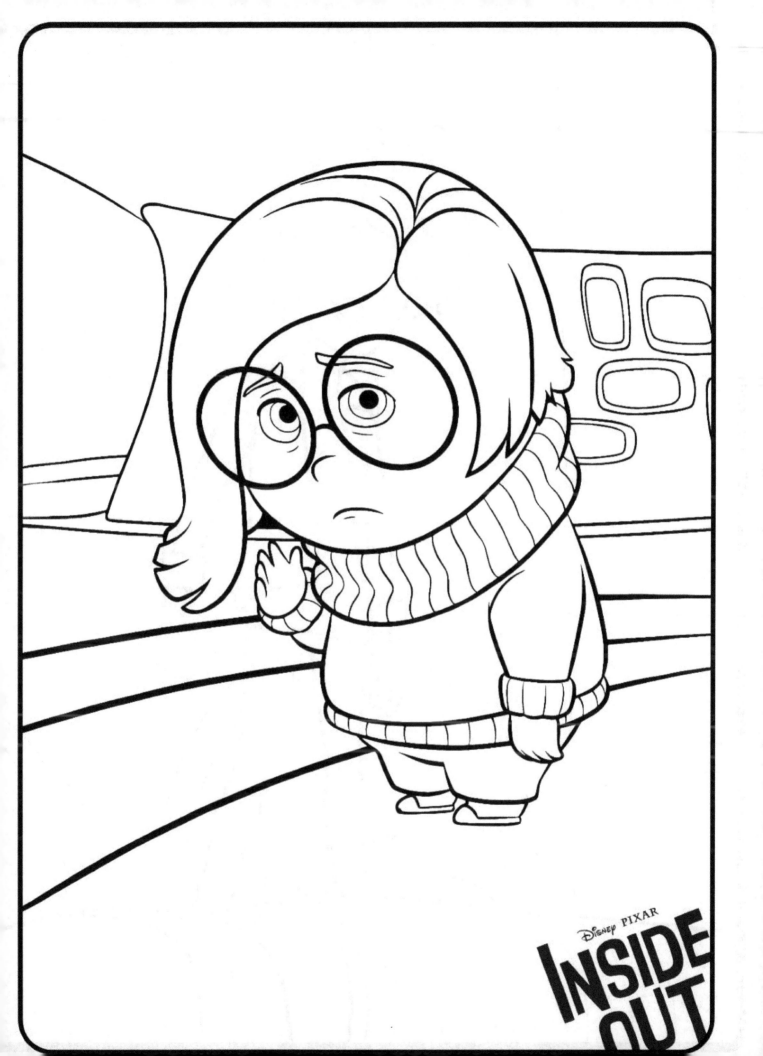

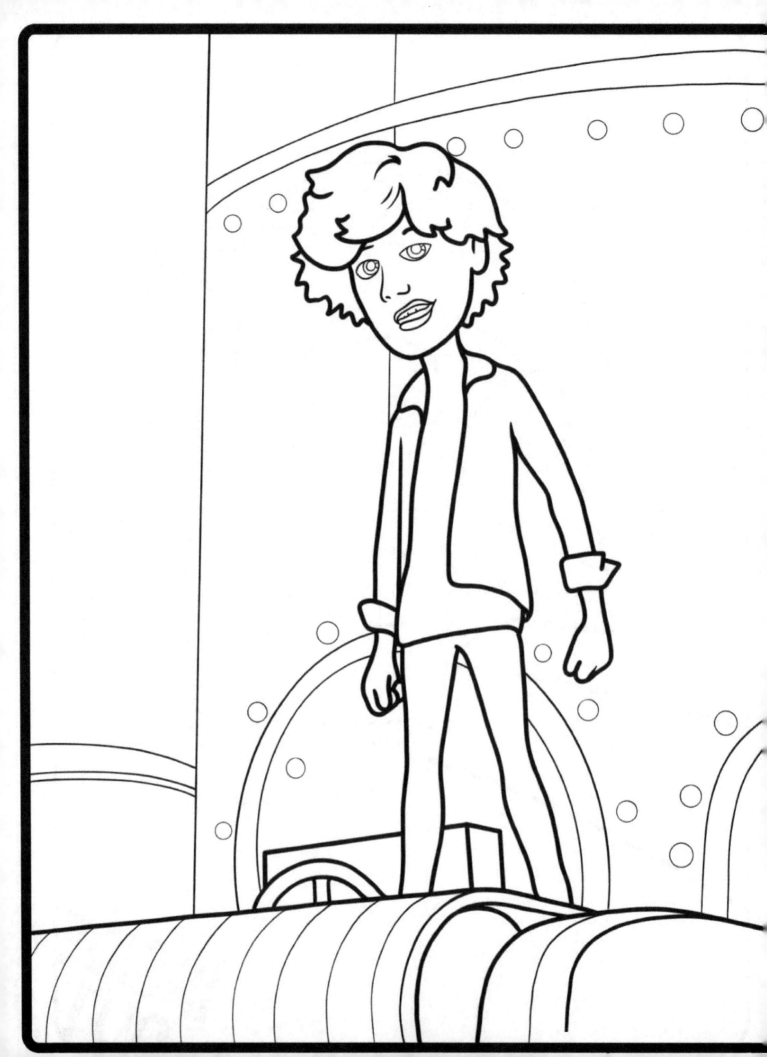

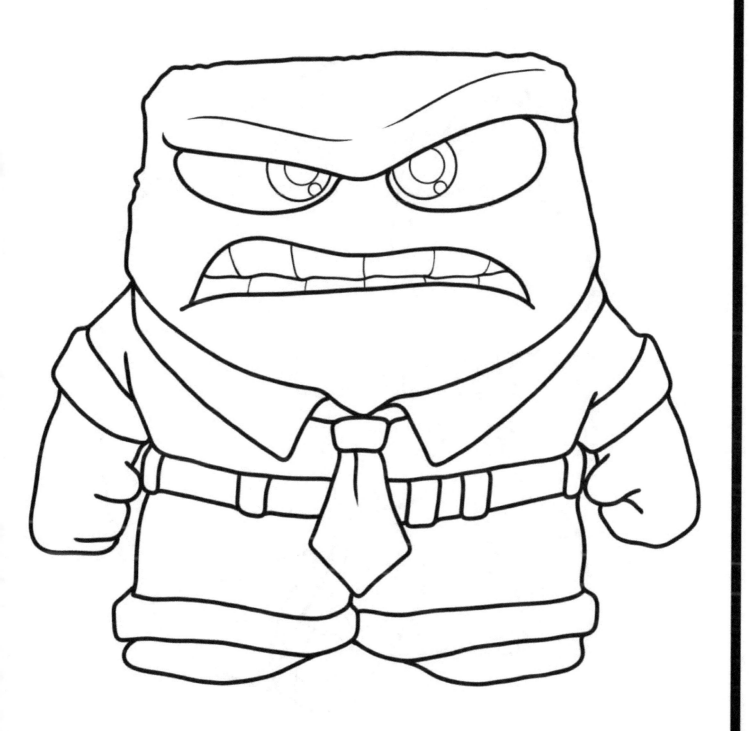

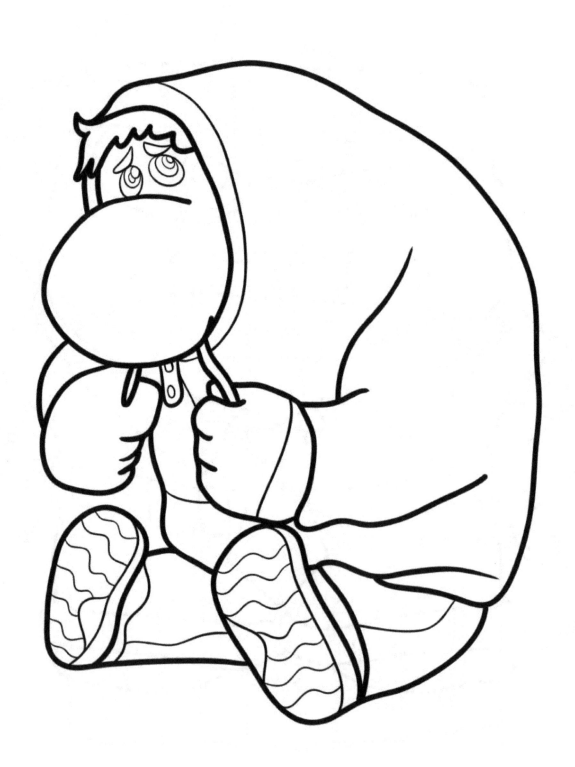

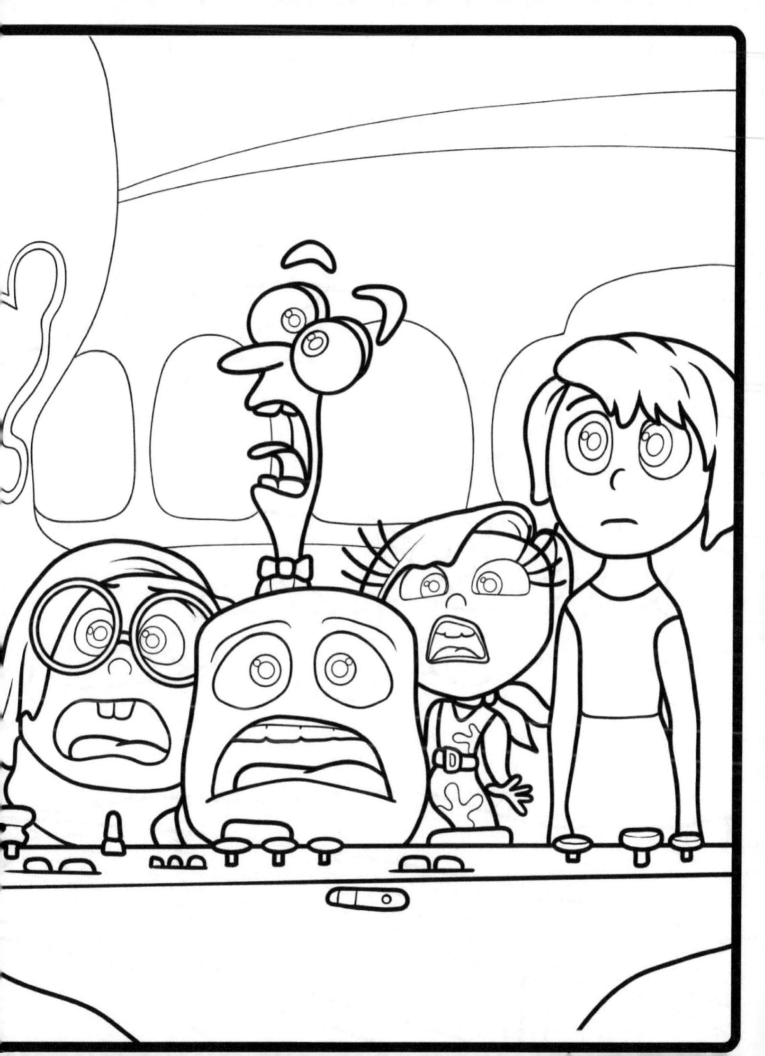

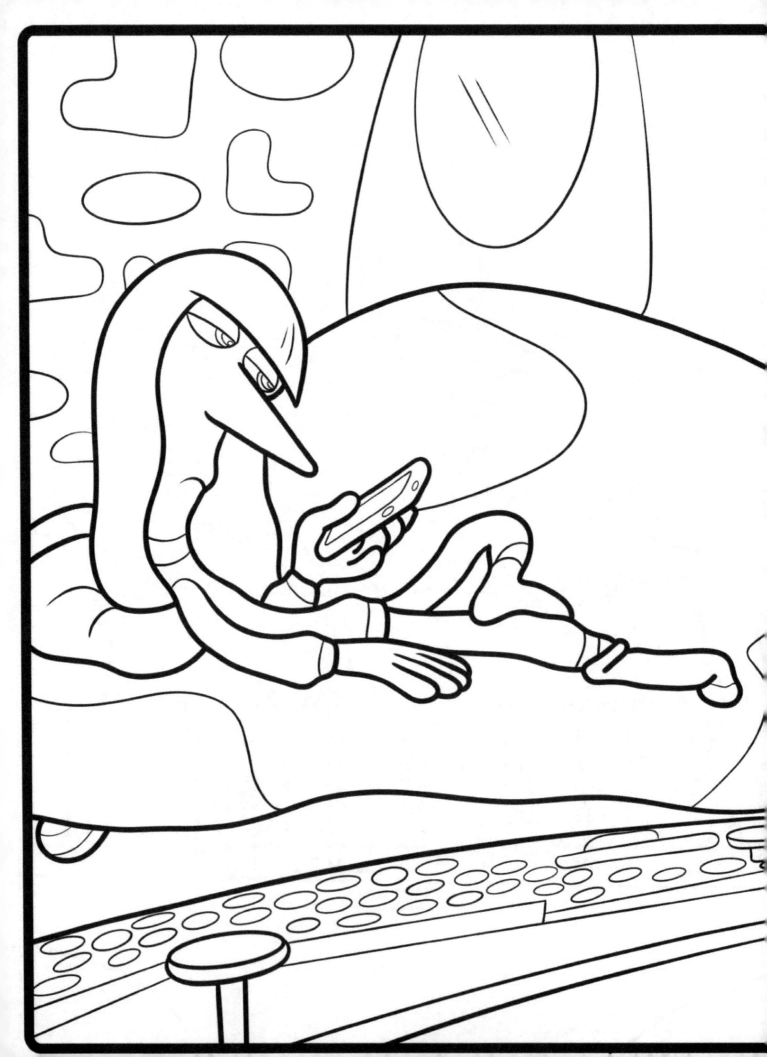

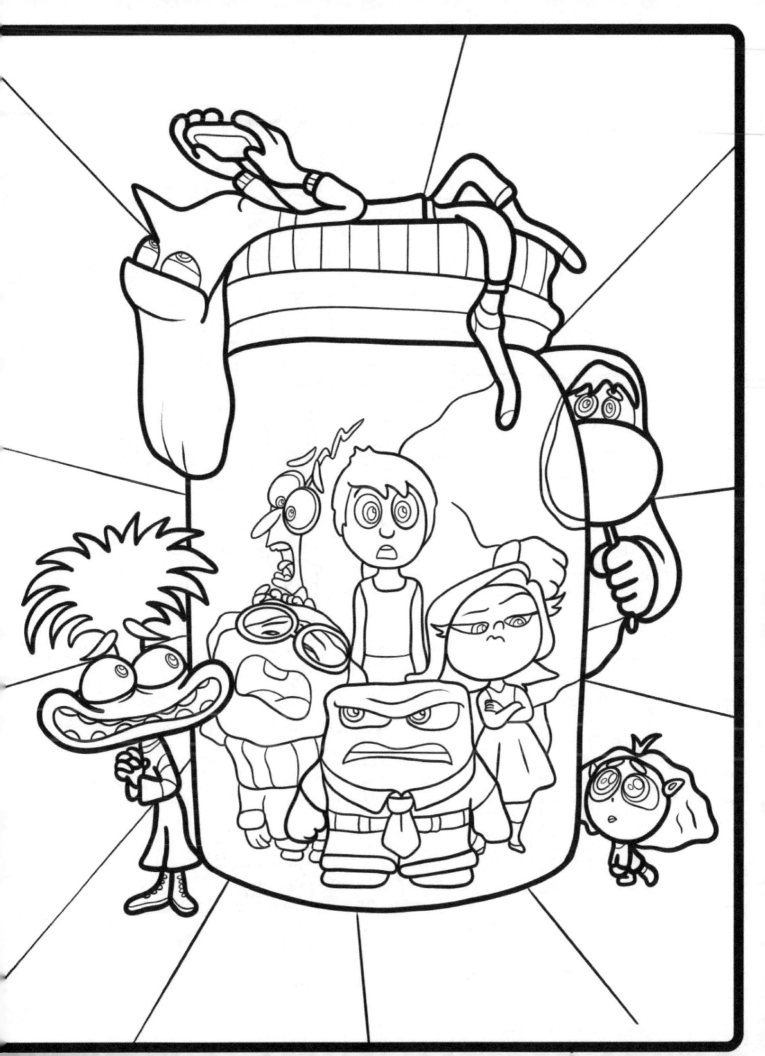

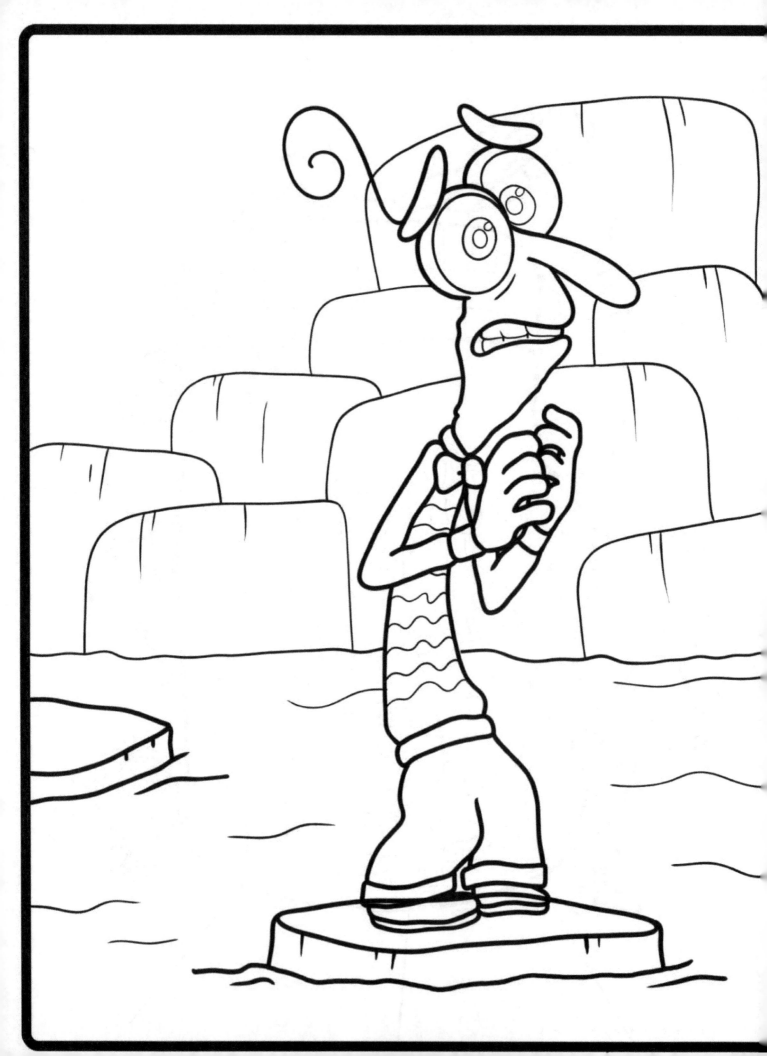

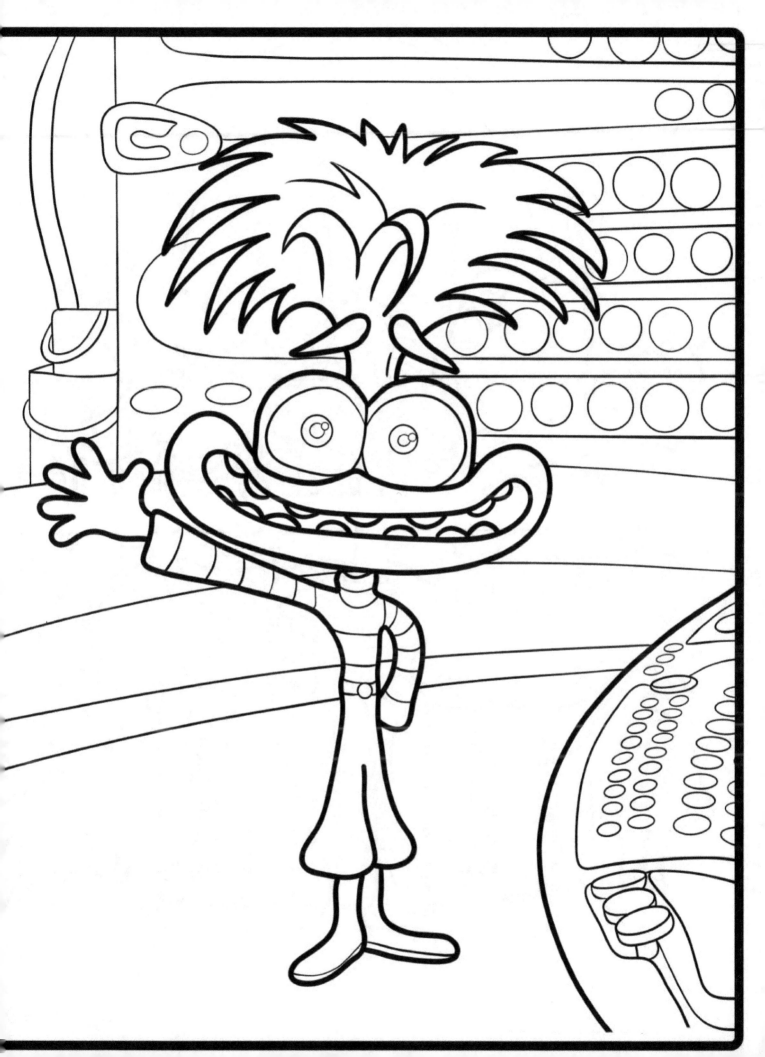

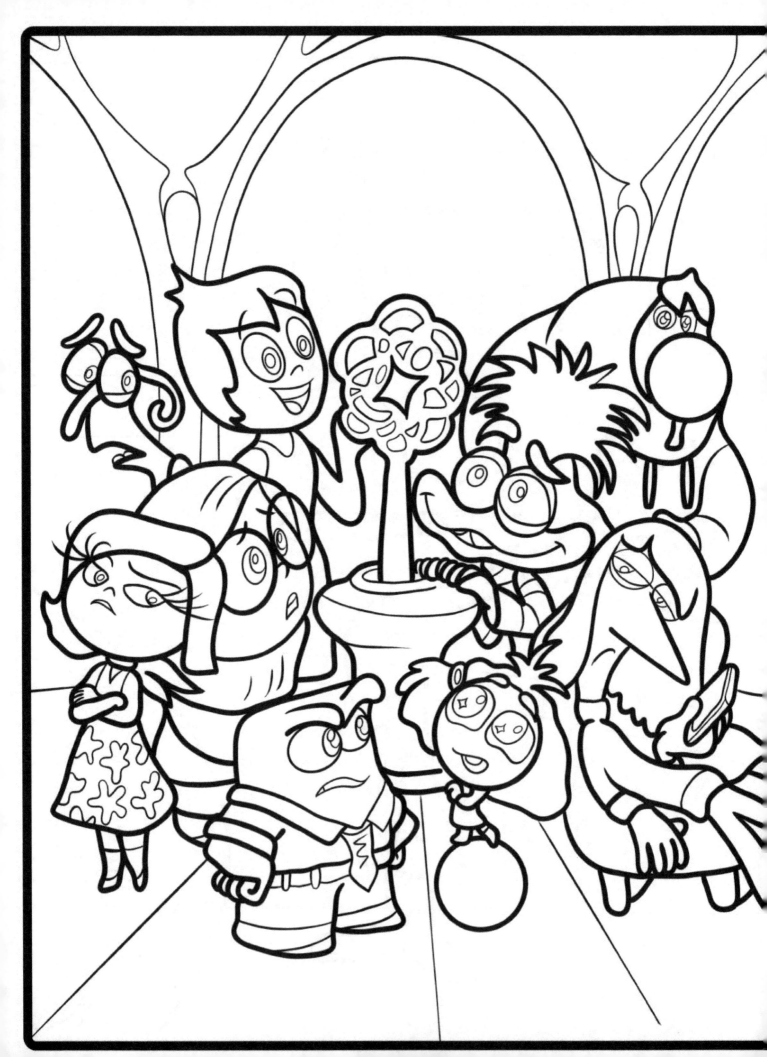

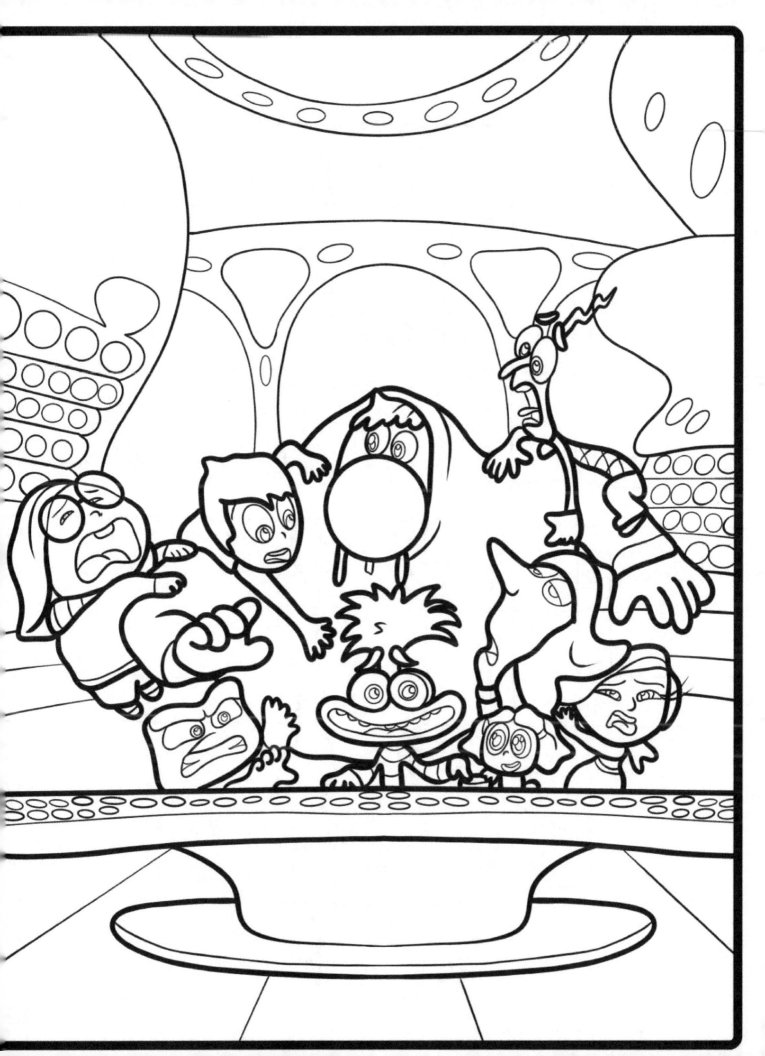

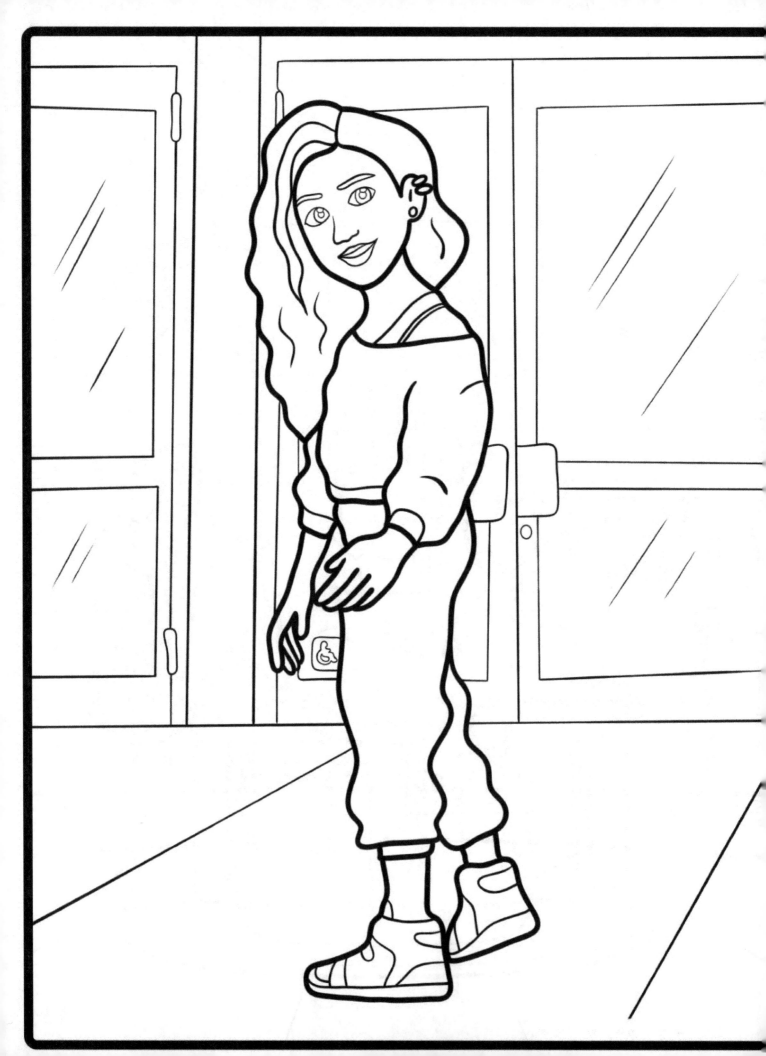

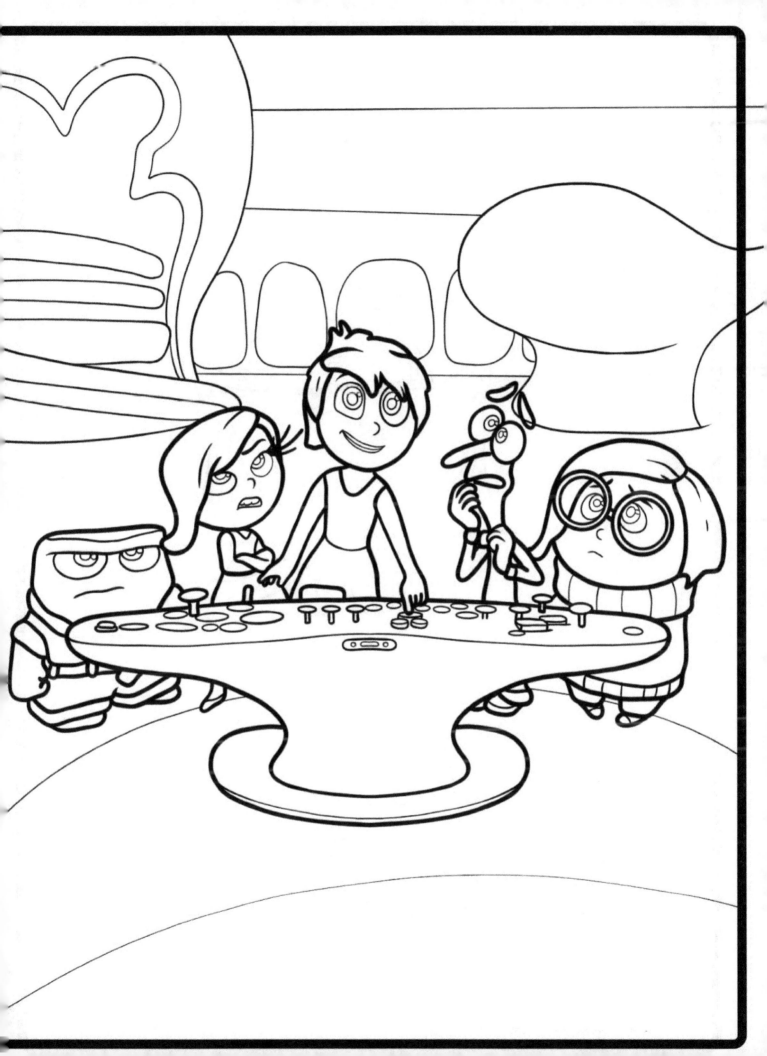

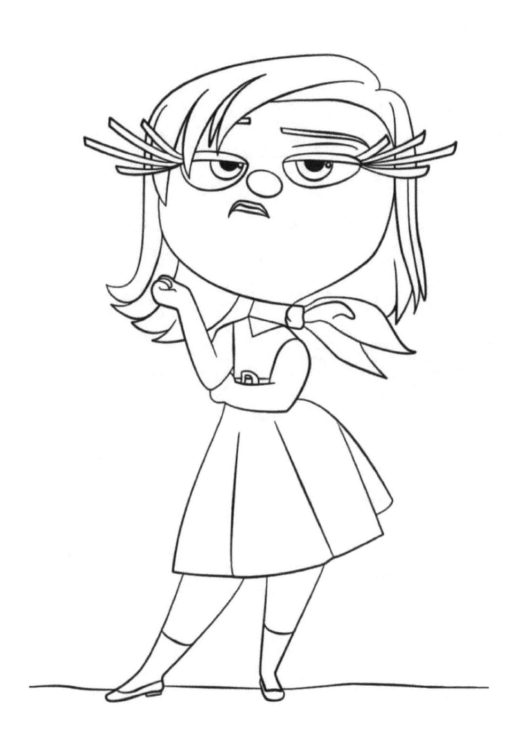

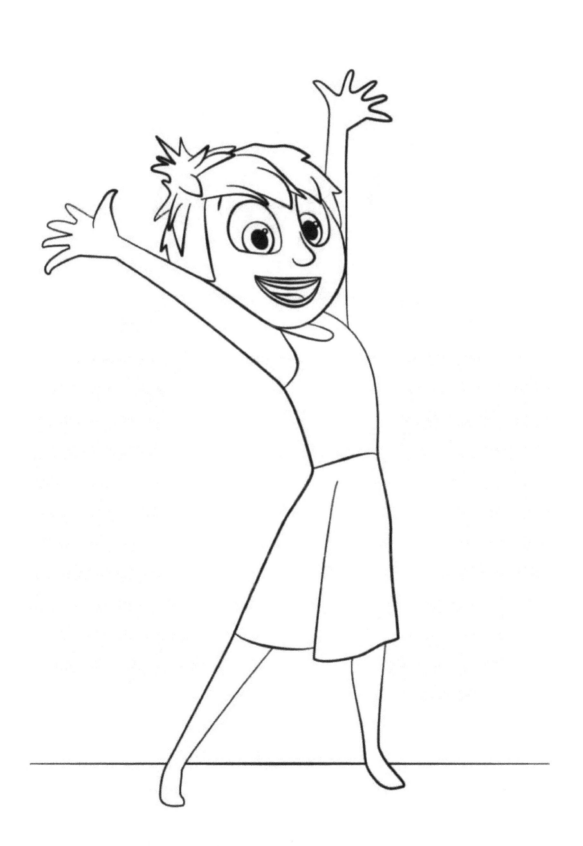

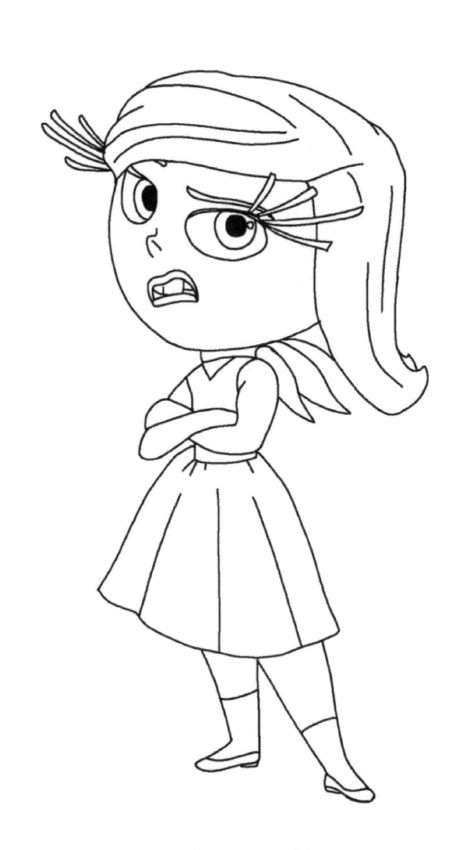

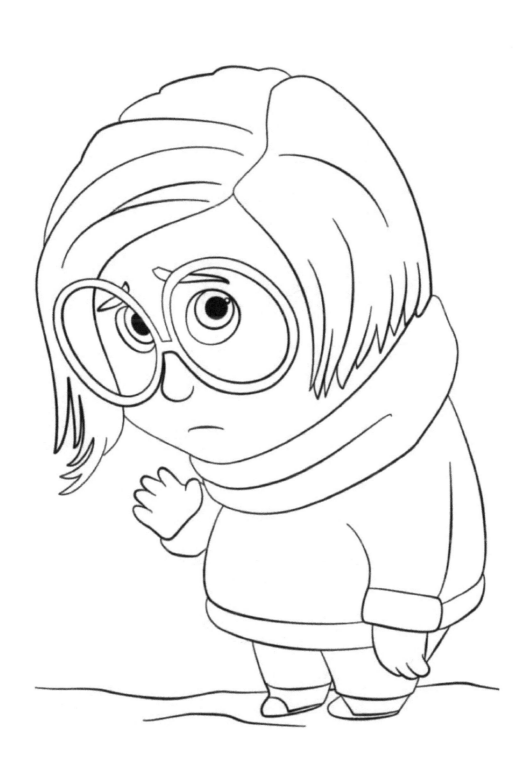

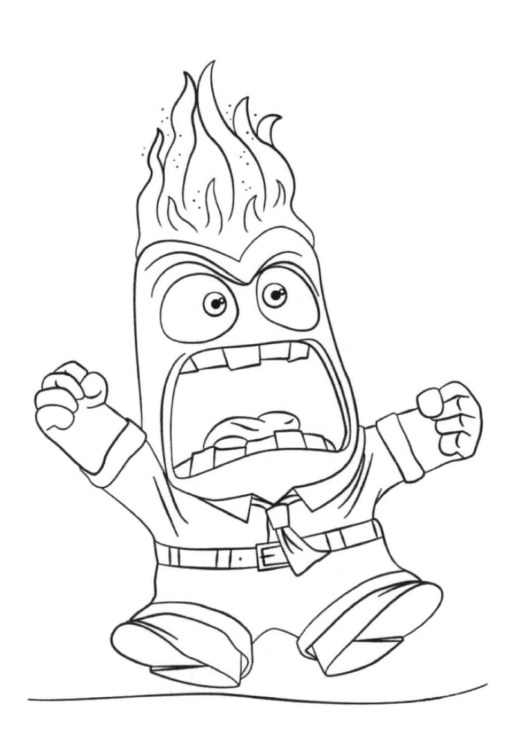

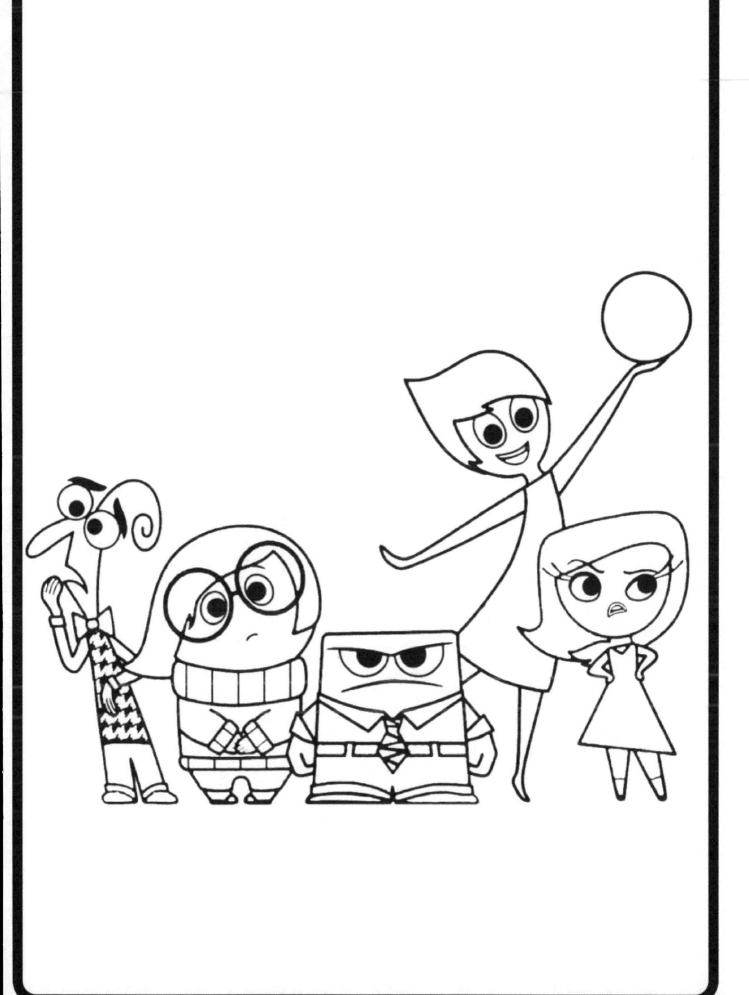

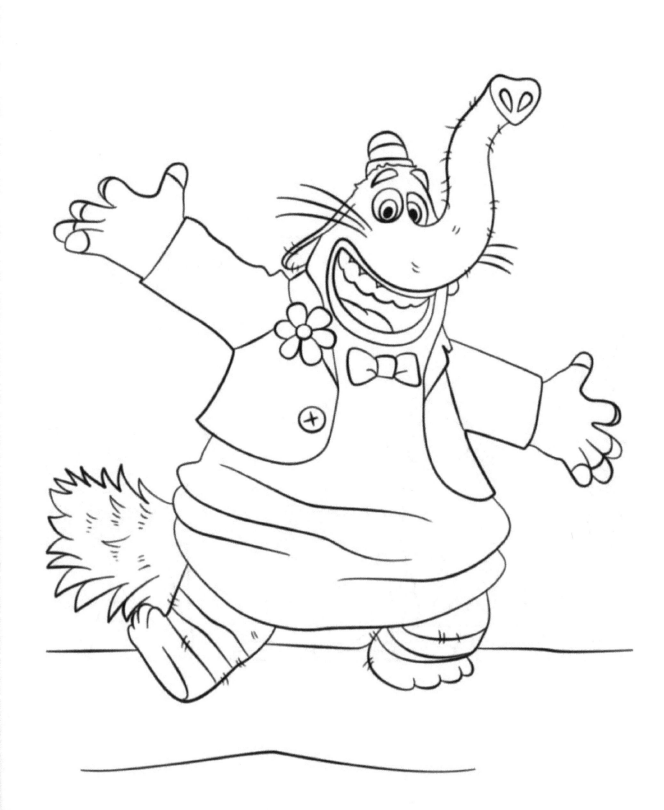

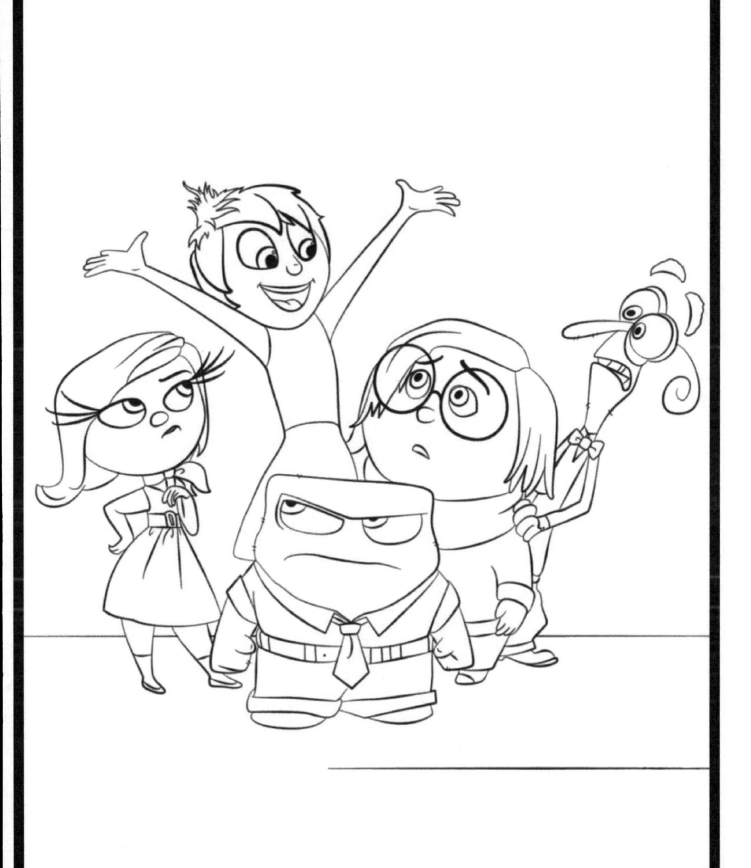

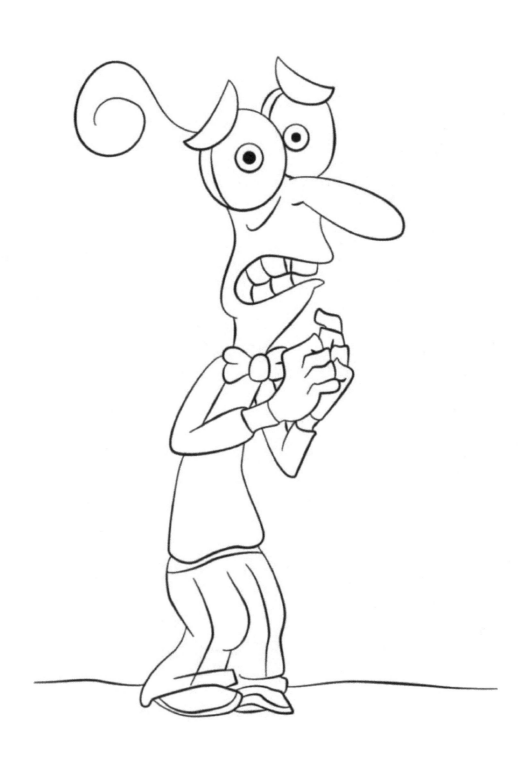

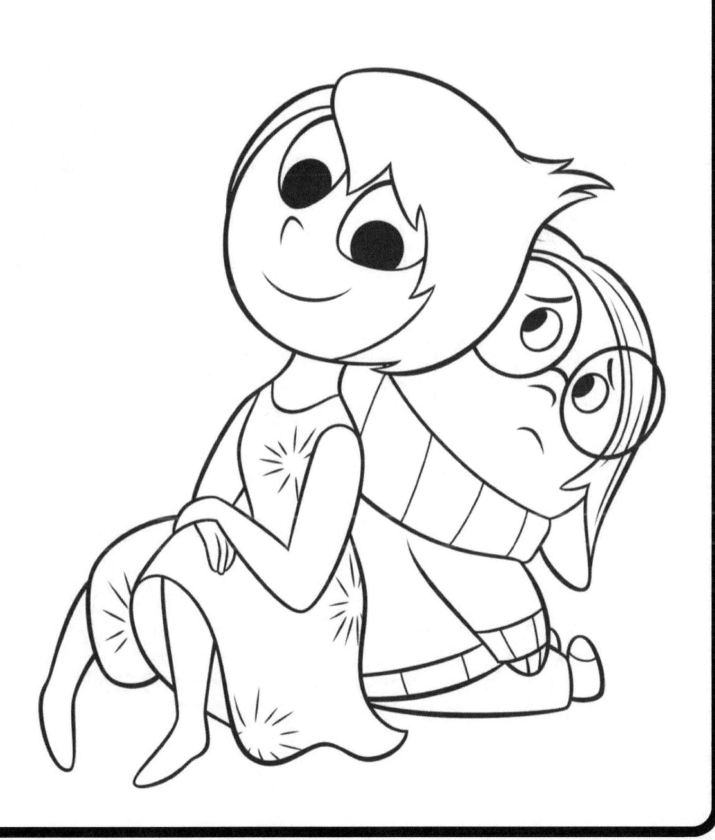

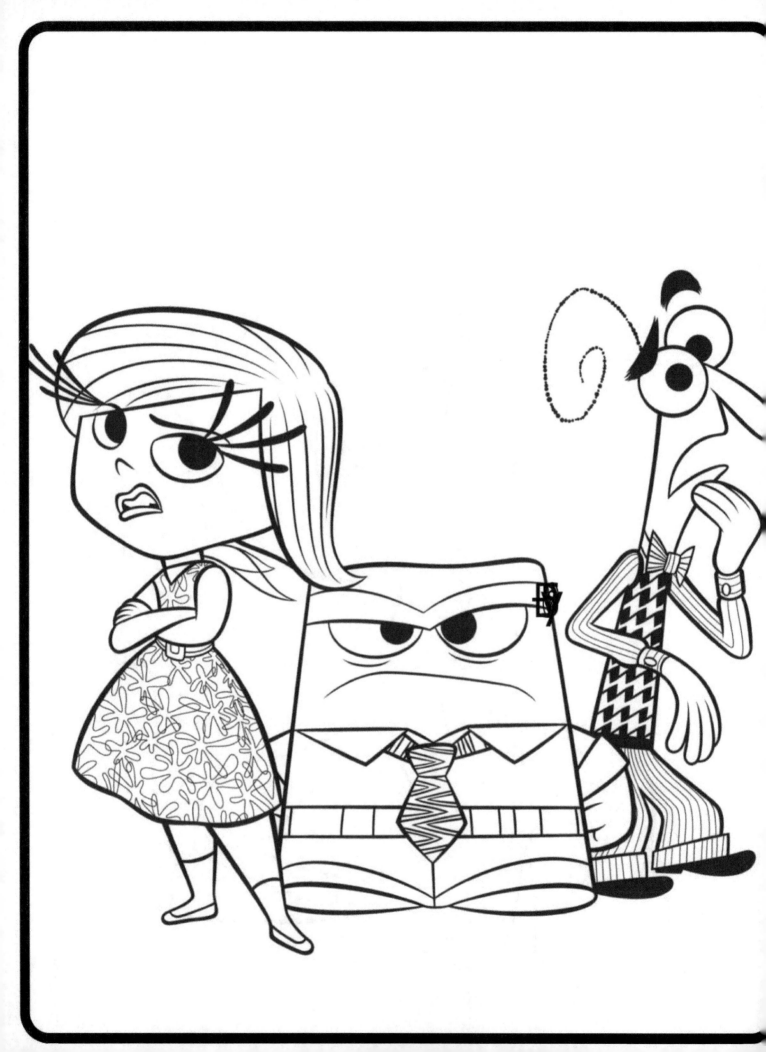

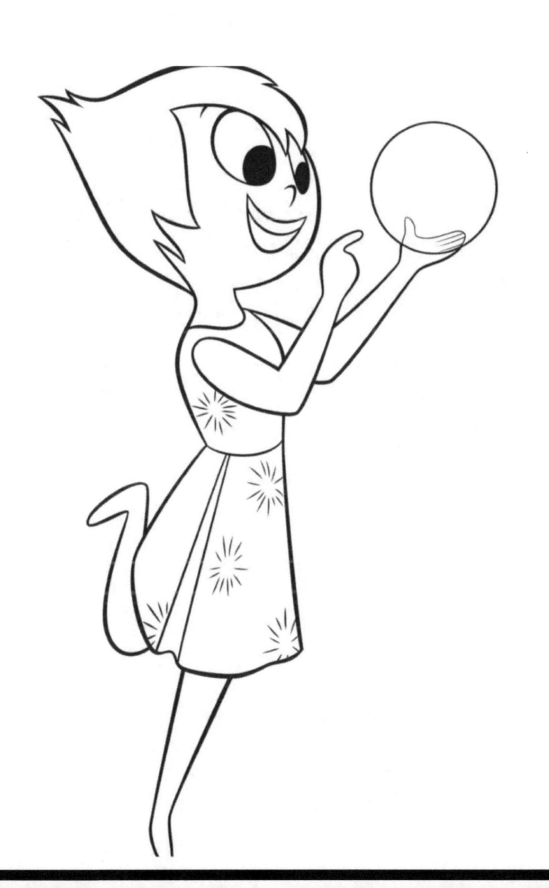

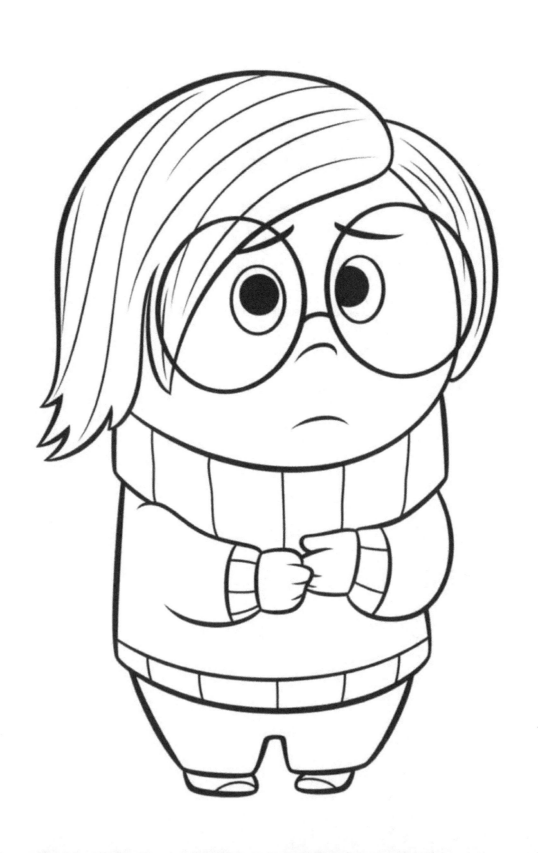

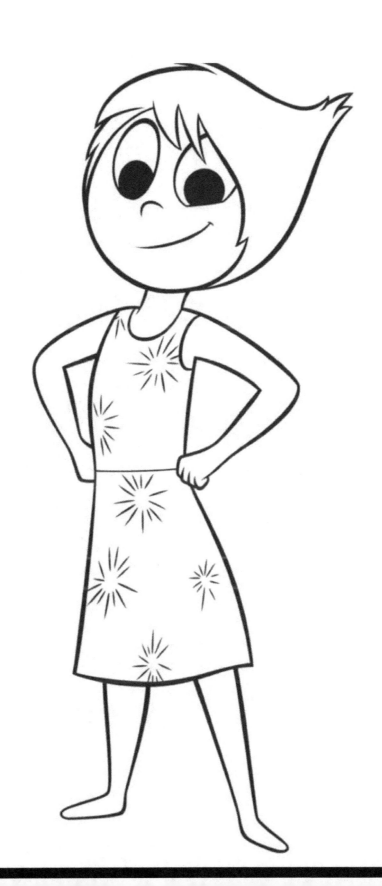

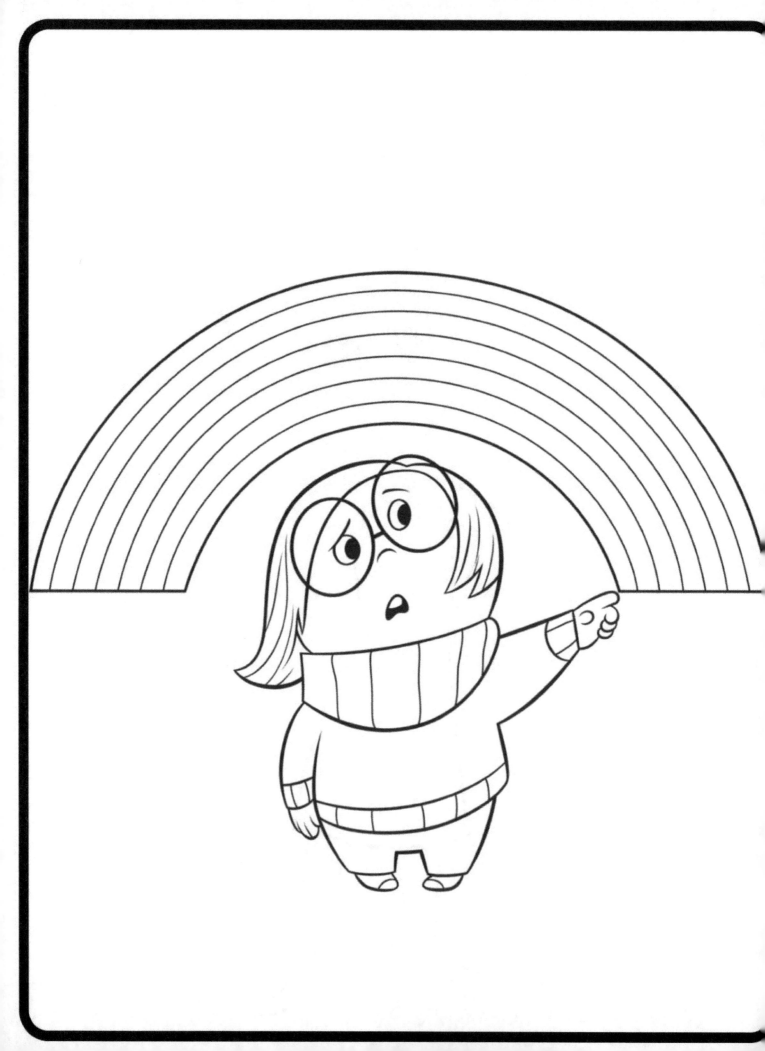

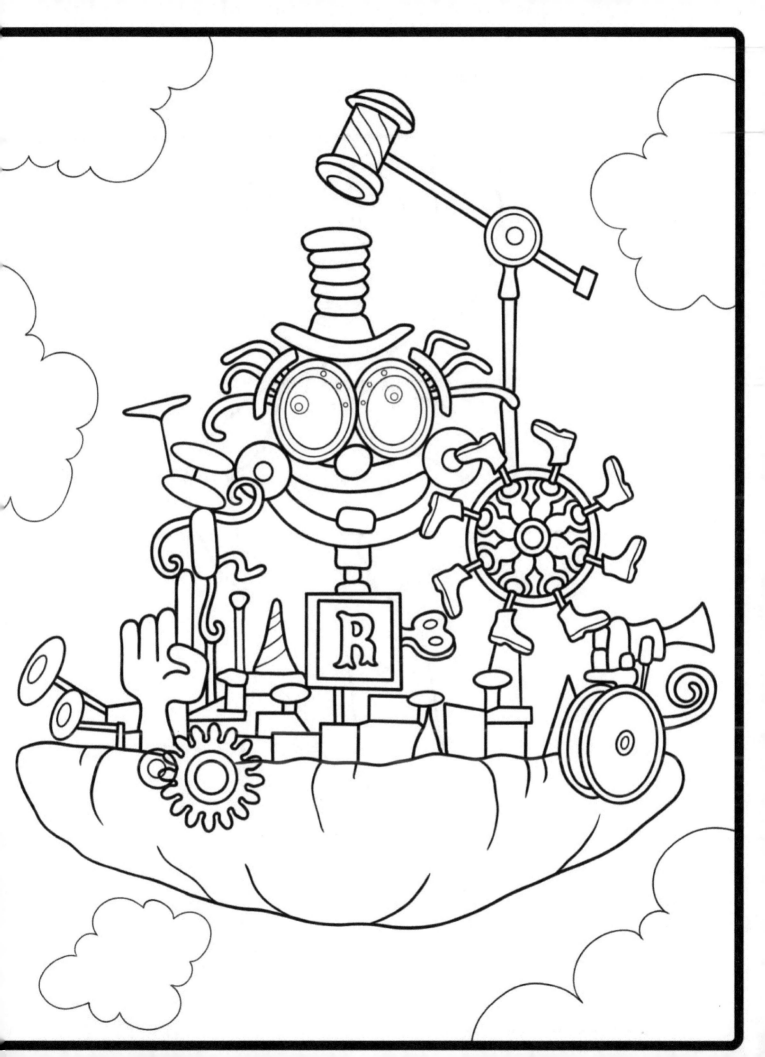

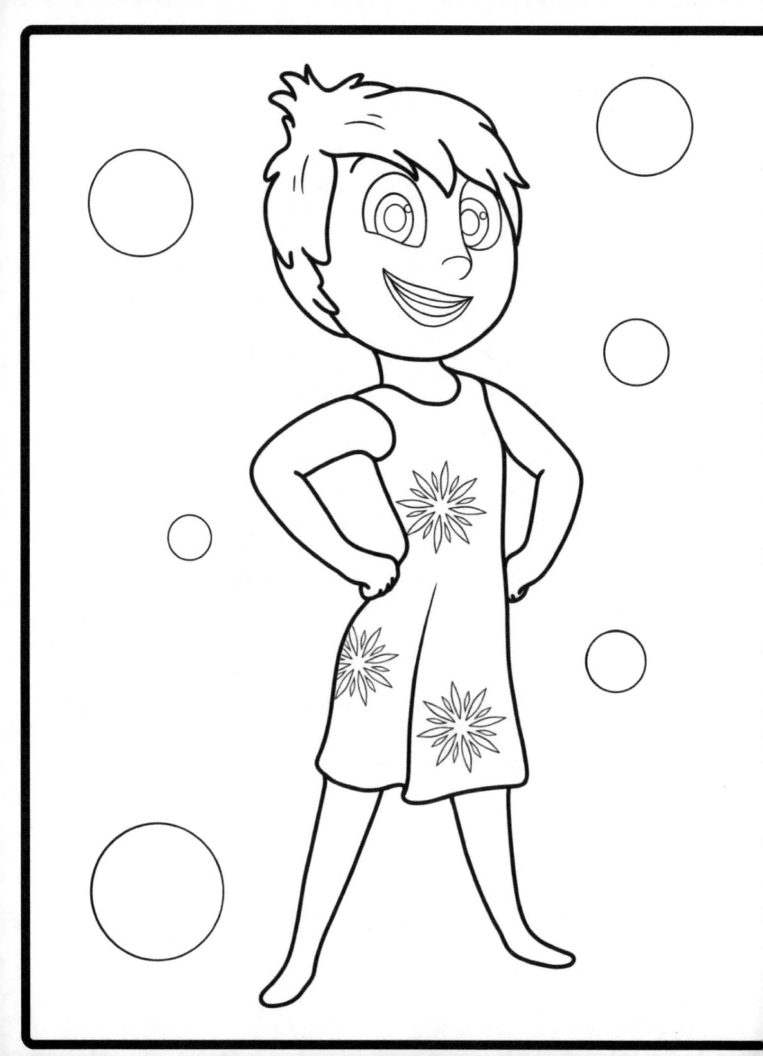

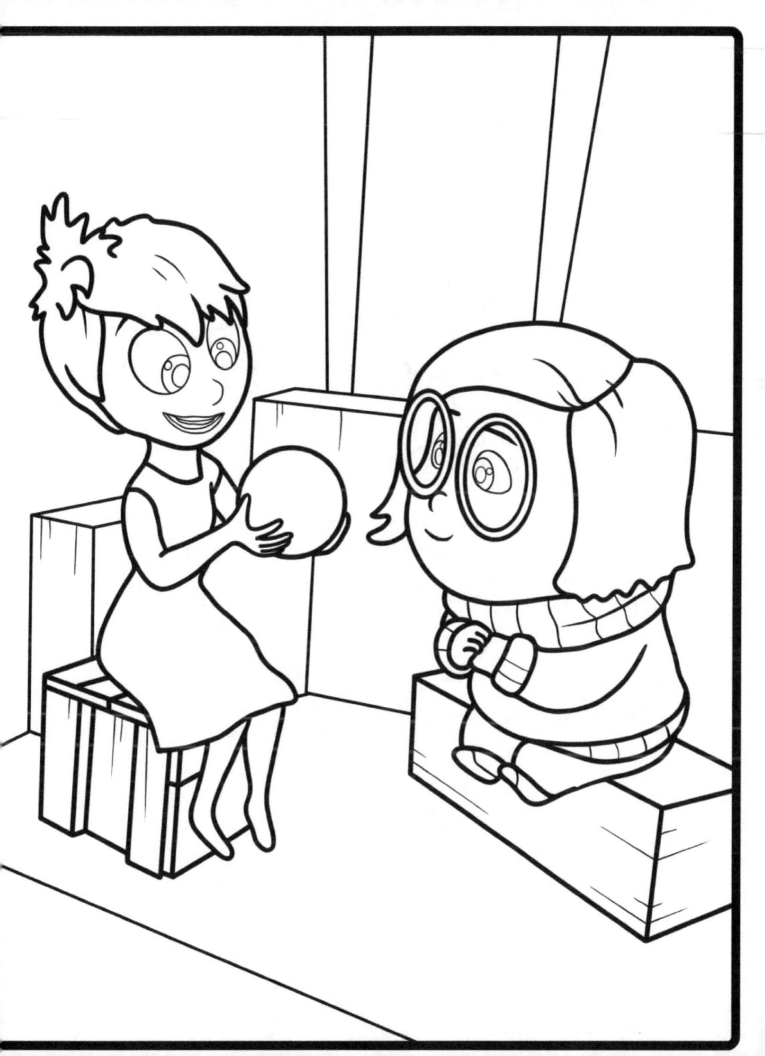

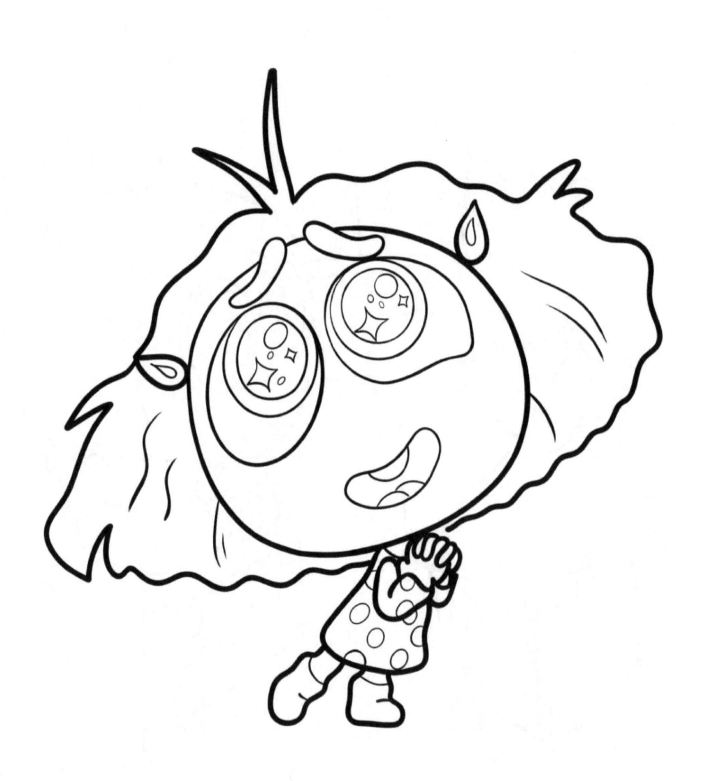

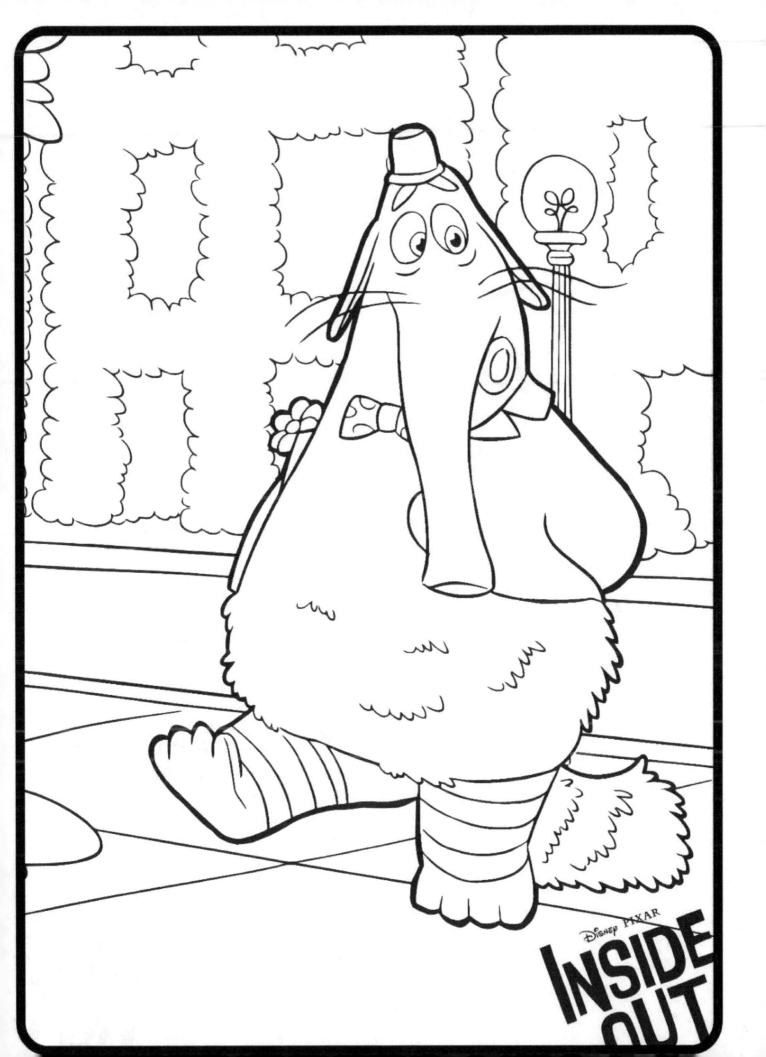

# Disgust    Fear

# Anger

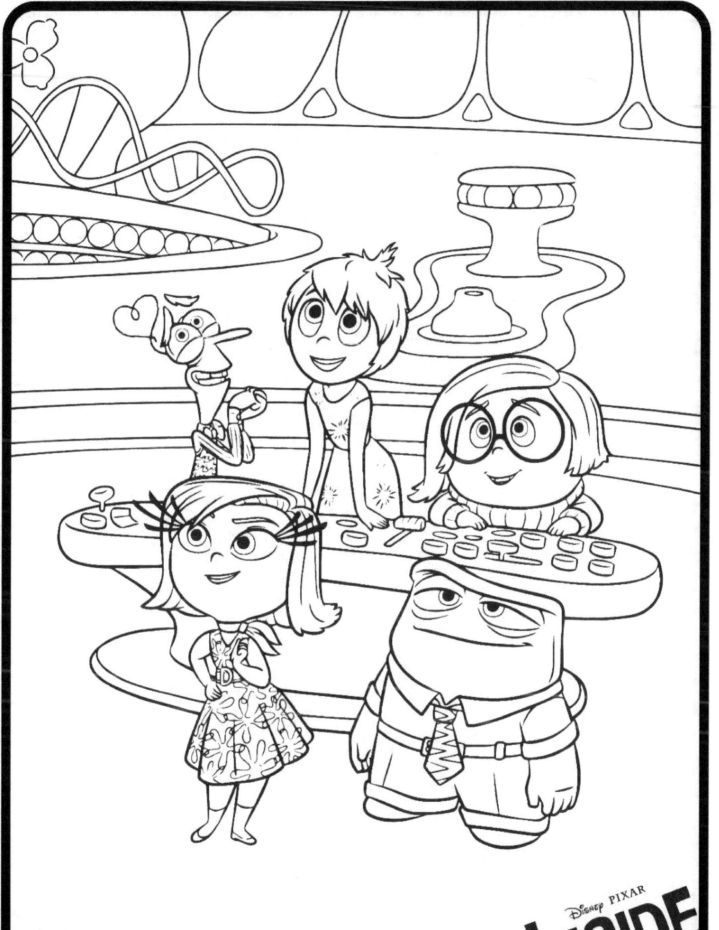

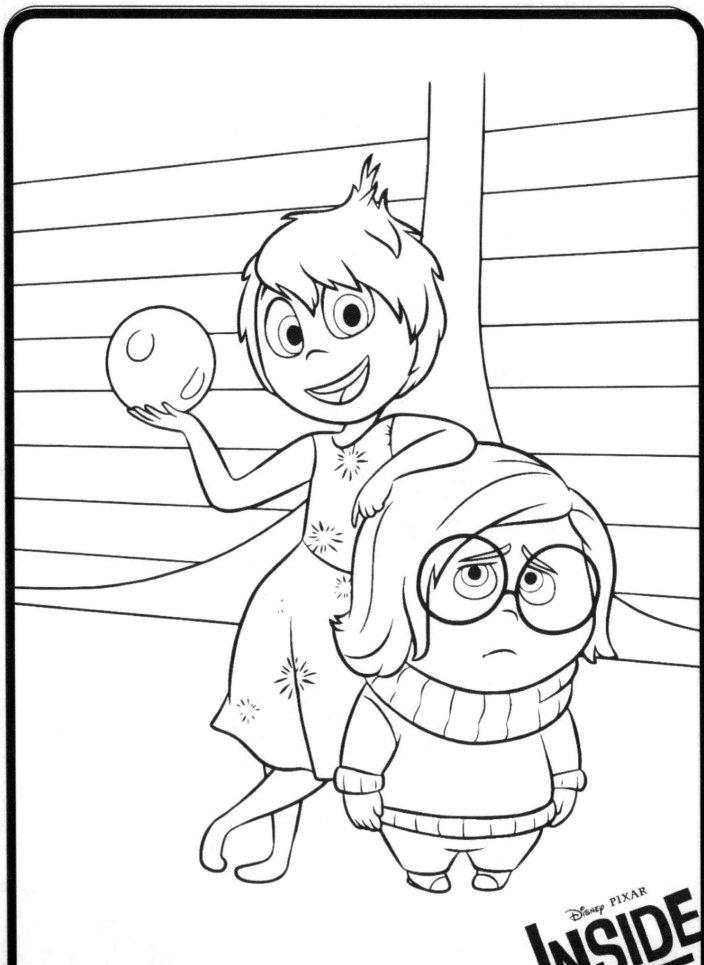

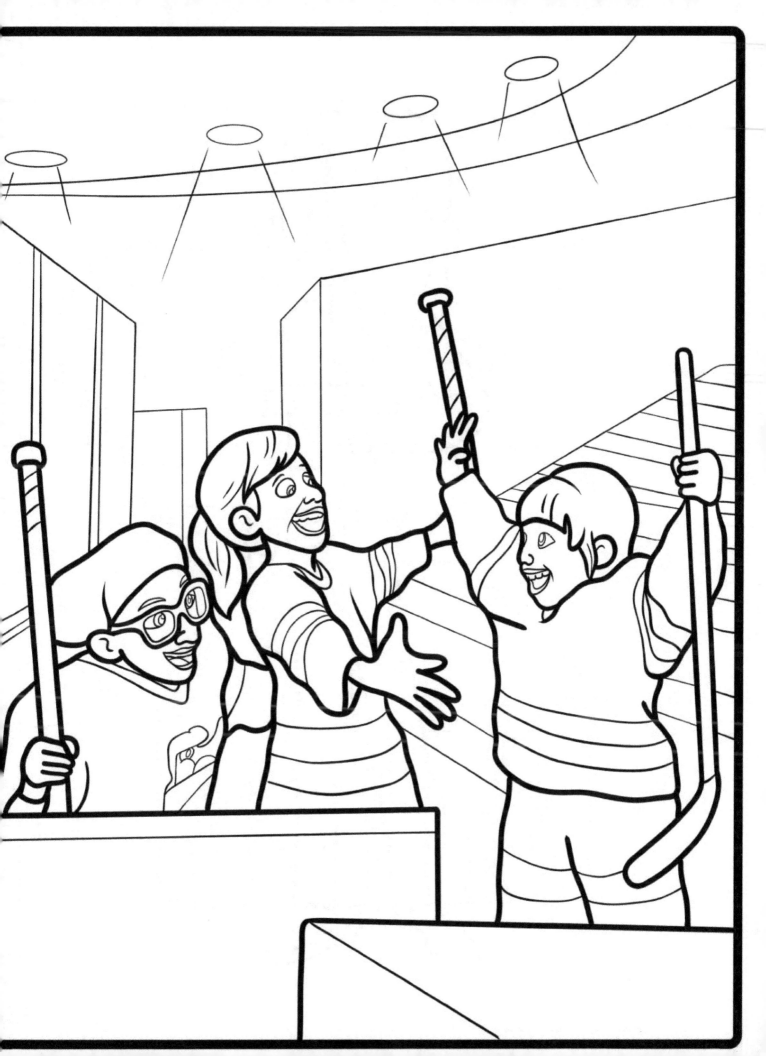

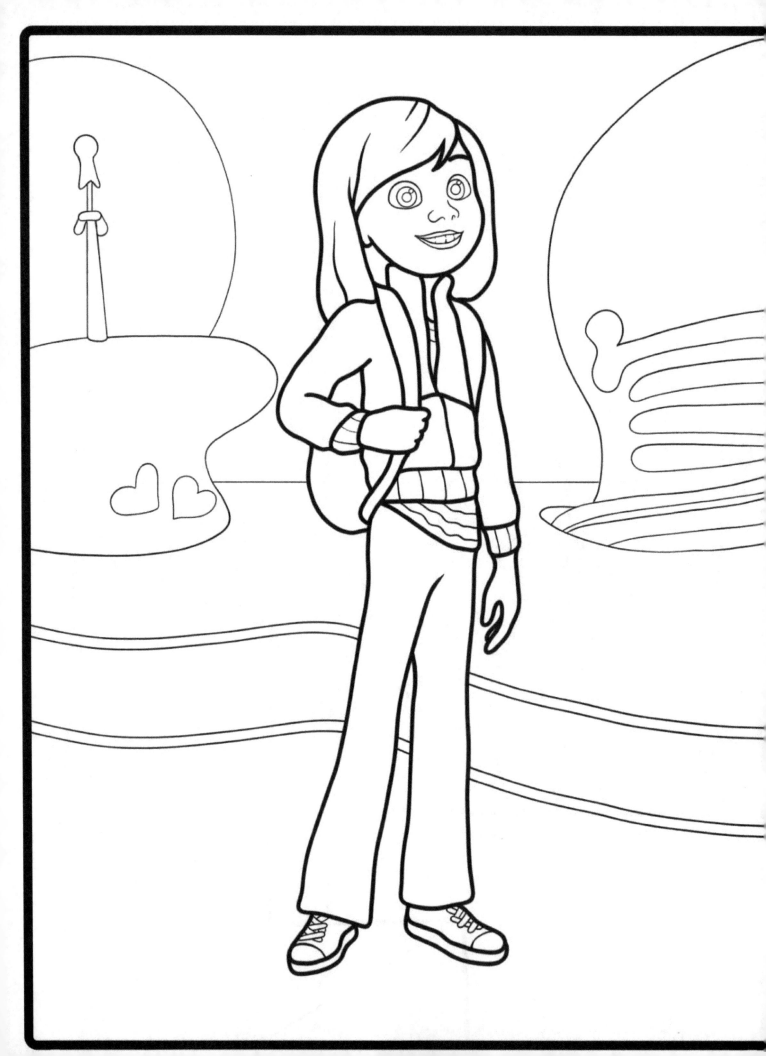

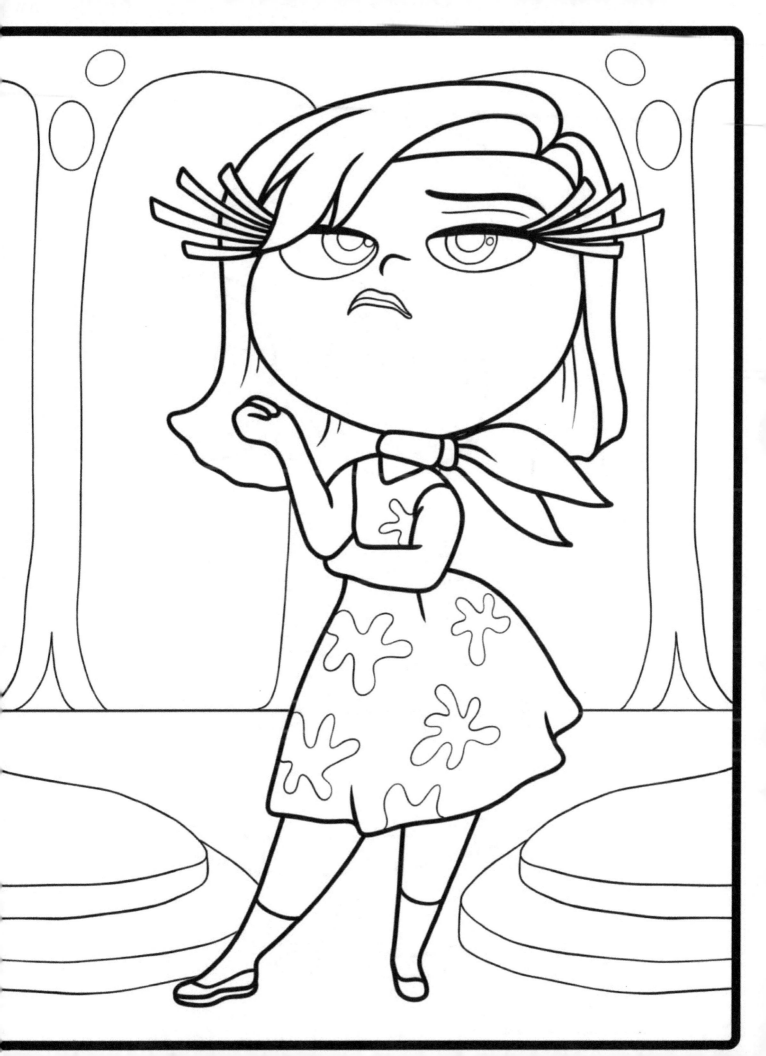

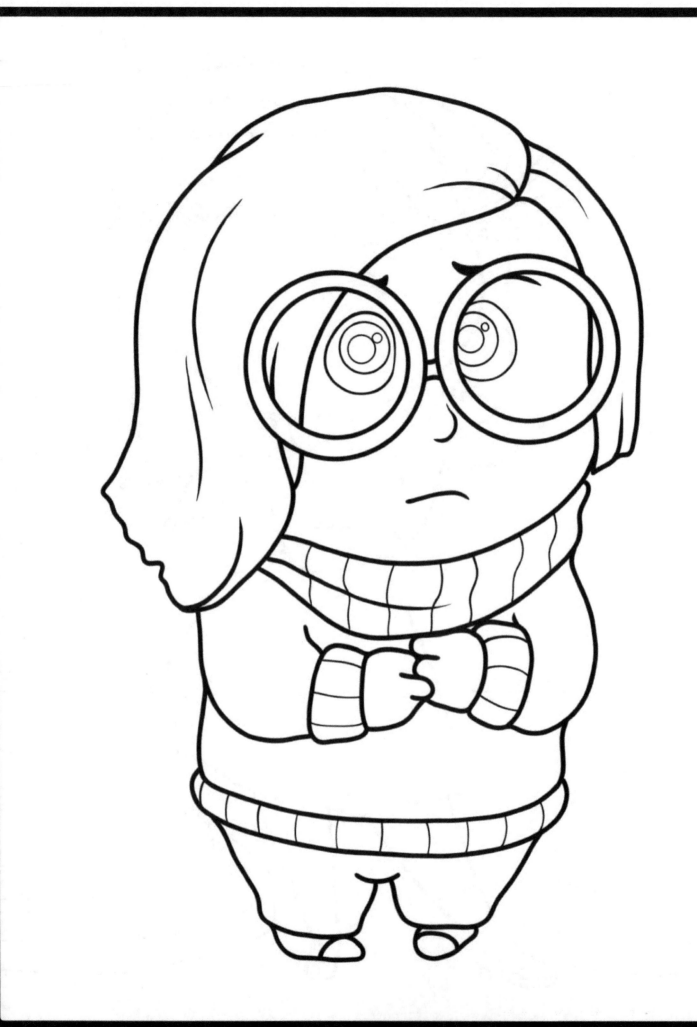

Printed in the USA
CPSIA information can be obtained
at www.ICGtesting.com
LVHW081147251024
794703LV00010B/229